"It is too rare to hav
us how to preach,
doing so. His discussion in *Eloquence* is remarkably nuanced,
where he calls for a combination of theological substance with
moving eloquence, as well as 'solemnity and unction.' What he
said a century ago is no less true now: 'Preaching is, at present,
out of touch with the time and does not meet its needs.' This volume will help us face the challenge of preaching in our own age."

—Tim Keller
Redeemer Presbyterian Church
New York City

"Many of us have been so impressed in recent years that Bavinck
as a theologian addresses our present-day context in marvelously
clear and compelling ways. Now we have further reason to be
grateful for his voice. In this wonderful book, Bavinck offers wise
counsel to preachers today—about style and content, about the
place of the sermon in the larger pattern of worship, and much
more! O Lord, move many preachers, and teachers of preaching,
to read this book!"

—Richard Mouw, President Emeritus and
Professor of Faith and Public Life
Fuller Theological Seminary

"The role of systematic theology in pastoral ministry must be to
do more than merely delimit the field of orthodoxy within which
a sermon ought always to remain. Good doctrine does more than
keep error out. It is itself a fertile source of creative insight as the
preacher submits to the text of Holy Scripture. In this latter role,
since its translation into English, Bavinck's four-volume *Reformed
Dogmatics* has been an invaluable tool for preachers in the Reformed tradition. However, when we ask how to bridge the gap
between the systematic-theological presentation of a particular
truth and the homiletic presentation of that truth from the text

of the Bible for the good of the church, the preacher is often left to struggle alone. James Eglinton has done the church a great service, therefore, in translating and editing Bavinck's reflections on preaching. His rhetorically beautiful *Eloquence*, his simple and clear sermon, "The World-Conquering Power of Faith," and his fascinating reflections on preaching and language are here combined with an invaluable introduction by Dr. Eglinton, to reveal a largely unknown side to Bavinck. Here we see a great systematician serving the church and modeling for us the way to combine doctrinal profundity with pastoral sympathy and homiletic simplicity."

—David Strain, Senior Pastor
First Presbyterian Church
Jackson, Mississippi

HERMAN
BAVINCK
on
PREACHING & PREACHERS

HERMAN
BAVINCK

on
PREACHING & PREACHERS

Translated and Edited by
JAMES P. EGLINTON

Herman Bavinck on Preaching & Preachers

© 2017 by Hendrickson Publishers Marketing, LLC
P. O. Box 3473
Peabody, Massachusetts 01961-3473
www.hendrickson.com

ISBN 978-1-61970-978-2

Printed in the United States of America

First Printing—September 2017

The image of Herman Bavinck used on the cover is courtesy of The Bavinck Institute in Grand Rapids, Michigan.

Cover design by Ron Piercey.

Library of Congress Cataloging-in-Publication Data

A catalog record for this title is available from the Library of Congress
Hendrickson Publishers Marketing, LLC ISBN 978-1-61970-978-2

CONTENTS

ACKNOWLEDGMENTS

I am grateful to a number of friends, colleagues, and students for their help in finishing this book. Sander Klaasse (PhD student, University of Edinburgh) was generous in giving up much time to check my translation of *Eloquence*. Marinus de Jong (PhD student, Theologische Universiteit Kampen) also provided help in clarifying the meaning of several archaic turns of phrase. Dr. Michael Bräutigam (Melbourne School of Theology) and Bruce Pass (PhD student, University of Edinburgh) have both offered valuable pointers in the translation of Bavinck's German quotations. Cory Brock (PhD student, University of Edinburgh) was kind enough to offer feedback on the introductory essay.

Some of the translation work was completed during a stay at Princeton Theological Seminary, which was enabled by the award of an Abraham Kuyper Visiting Scholarship. Accordingly, I express my thanks to the seminary's Abraham Kuyper Center for Public Theology. The project also benefited from the outstanding services of the Historisch Documentatiecentrum at the Vrije Universiteit Amsterdam, where I was able to work on Bavinck's unpublished materials. Thanks are also due to Marinus and Wibbina de Jong for their hospitality during that research trip. I am indebted to Greg Parker at Hendrickson Publishers, whose kindness and enthusiasm for the project played a significant role in moving it toward publication.

This book is dedicated to George Harinck—a mentor, and a friend. I acknowledge all mistakes and shortcomings as my own.

Dr. James Eglinton
Edinburgh
September 2016

INTRODUCTION

In the course of the last decade, Herman Bavinck's *Reformed Dogmatics*[1] has become a standard text in the theological diet of Reformed and evangelical preachers in the Anglophone world. Rigorous in his grounding in Scripture, constant in recourse to the tri-unity of God, and intentionally Christocentric in each dogmatic movement, Bavinck has come to typify how an emerging generation of preachers views the theological task. He is increasingly the theologian to whom they turn in looking for dogmatic formation. In their weekly endeavors, however, those preachers are crafting and delivering sermons, rather than dogmatic treatises. By and large, their task is homiletical. While Bavinck's writings on dogmatics might enrich their appreciation of the exegesis of Scripture, historical theology, and critically appreciative engagement with modern theology, the question remains of how exactly this translates into how they prepare and deliver sermons.

This book exists because there is a curious gap between Bavinck the theologian and the preachers who read him in the present day. I describe this gap as curious because Bavinck himself was also a preacher. He preached for the first time in 1878, aged twenty-four, and continued to preach regularly until his death some forty-two years later. However, how Bavinck preached, or what and how he thought about the act of preaching and the person of the preacher, are largely unknown to the preachers who read his *Reformed Dogmatics* today. This is so due to linguistic factors, in that his writings on preaching were previously untranslated, this being coupled with the relative difficulty of accessing those sources for much of the twentieth century.

It is certainly unusual that a preacher like Bavinck would go on to exert such influence on a generation of preachers who themselves are largely unacquainted with him in precisely that capacity. The realization of this immediately prompts intriguing questions: What kind of a preacher was Bavinck? How did he try to form his students as preachers? Neo-Calvinism is often associated with a particular form of sermon content. The redemptive-historical hermeneutics exemplified by Geerhardus Vos provides much neo-Calvinist preaching with a particular way of connecting biblical texts to the gospel of Christ, and is closely linked to the notion of "neo-Calvinist preaching." However, the question remains: Is there such a thing as a distinctively *neo-Calvinist* homiletical method or style of preaching or view of the person of the preacher? What will emerge in the pulpit if the broader theological enterprise found in the *Reformed Dogmatics* (rather than simply a particular form of biblical hermeneutics) takes root in the study?

In large part, this book has developed in an effort to explore and answer those questions. The first impulse to do so came from the Belgian Dominican theologian Edward Schillebeeckx, whose work *For the Sake of the Gospel* opens with the following statement: "Faith, theology and preaching are difficult to separate, certainly for a theologian. But one can discover what a theologian really thinks from her or his preaching."[2] While there is certainly much to meditate upon regarding the intertwined nature of faith, theology, and preaching in the person of the Christian preacher, Schillebeeckx's reminder carries a pointed emphasis: a great deal about a particular theologian's *theology* can be learned from his *preaching*—but such learning can be lost when looking only for theology in that theologian's dogmatic work. For Schillebeeckx, this is because good preaching *is* the intersection of dogma, moral theology, the preacher's own life of faith, and the lives of those to whom the gospel is preached. These factors converge in the act of preaching the gospel, which binds preacher and congregation. "Pure preaching," Schillebeeckx argued elsewhere, "demands not only constant contact with the living God in prayer and human experience, but also the sustained practice of going back to theological sources."[3] As such, it stands to reason that a theologian's preaching will reveal a great deal about his theology.

This insight cannot be applied to every theologian, as not all theologians are also preachers. However, in the case of someone who is both a theologian and a preacher, as is true of Bavinck, Schillebeeckx's point is useful: engage with Bavinck the preacher, and you will likely acquire a more richly textured grasp of his theology. This assertion may well be striking to many of Bavinck's Anglophone readers, insofar as they are the preachers who know him as a theologian. What would happen if they became reacquainted with Bavinck as a fellow preacher? Would it help them more deeply consider their own theological commitments in the light of their preaching, or their preaching in the light of those commitments?

This book tries to encourage engagement with these questions by offering translations of Bavinck's key texts on preaching and preachers, and his only published sermon. As well as being an additional resource in the growing corpus of Bavinck texts available in English, it aims to stimulate preachers who read his *Reformed Dogmatics* in their own reflective practice. In *Reformed Dogmatics*, Bavinck sets out to "think God's thoughts after him."[4] In this book's translated offerings, he tries to articulate those thoughts through, and in relation to, the preaching of the word of God.

HERMAN BAVINCK: BIOGRAPHY OF A PREACHER

Herman Bavinck (1854–1921) was born on December 13, 1854, as the son of a preacher in the Dutch town of Hoogeveen. His father, Jan Bavinck (1826–1909), was a Reformed pastor originally from Bentheim, in Lower Saxony. His mother was Gezina Magdalena Bavinck (née Holland, 1827–1900). The second of seven children, Herman was born into the theologically conservative, ecclesiastically separatist Christian Reformed Church (*Christelijke Gereformeerde Kerk*). After completing his high school education,

Herman enrolled as a student at the Theological School in Kampen, the town where his father was then a Christian Reformed pastor. Jan Bavinck's years in Kampen were heavily invested in his preaching ministry: "On the Lord's Day there were three occasions to preach to be fulfilled, and in the winter there was also one occasion added in the week."[5] Although one of these sermons was preached by a faculty member from the Theological School, Jan Bavinck was responsible for the rest. Evidently, he found great personal fulfilment in this work:

> Oh, I still vividly remember some occasions, especially in the evenings by gaslight, how quietly and attentively a great crowd could listen to the preaching, and seemed to devour the words of the preacher! There was hunger and thirst for the Word of God and the words of life were food and drink for hungry and thirsty souls. I may believe that my work in those days was not without fruit and blessing.[6]

After one year as a student in Kampen—in a context where his father's preaching impressed a warm, personal, and experiential piety upon students and faculty alike—Herman made the daring decision to continue his studies at the aggressively modernist theological faculty at the University of Leiden. The theology on offer at Leiden could scarcely have been more different from the Christian Reformed seminary in Kampen. The Leiden school viewed Christianity as a now redundant phase in the evolution of human civilization, the church as something that could now be replaced by the secular state, and the Bible as a text to be studied along humanistic lines.

Why did the teenage Bavinck make such a move? Although he experienced a crisis of faith while at Leiden (from which he eventually emerged), his choice to study in Leiden was not an abandonment of the orthodox Reformed theology of his upbringing. Rather, his choice was motivated in part by his search for a more rigorous academic training in theology than could be offered in Kampen at that time. Alongside this, Bavinck was motivated by the presence of the Christian Reformed pastor Johannes Hendricus

Donner (1824–1903) in Leiden. Bavinck's student journal notes that he decided to move to Leiden having heard Donner—at that time, perhaps his denomination's most outstanding preacher—speak on missions in Kampen.[7]

Between 1874 and 1880 at Leiden, Bavinck studied under the likes of Johannes Scholten and Abraham Kuenen—the then superstars of Dutch academic theology. There, he admired the scientific approach of his professors, though he often found himself in deep disagreement with their presuppositions and doctrinal conclusions. During this time, he was profoundly influenced by Donner's sermons. Indeed, the early entries from Bavinck's Leiden-era journal devote far more attention to Donner than to his university professors.[8] As far as Bavinck's thoughts on these sermons can be reconstructed through his notes on them, they appealed to him because they were exegetically oriented and engaged explicitly with themes relevant to Bavinck's situation at that time—modernism and its fruits, the difference between faith and unbelief, and the contrast of sin and grace. The book of sermons on the sufferings of Christ published by Donner in 1883, *Lichtstralen van den kandelaar des woords*, provides a clear impression of the kind of preaching enjoyed by Bavinck in his student years.[9] The sermons in that collection focus on expounding the biblical text and are thoroughly evangelical in character. In terms of rhetoric, they lay claim on the hearer's attention by posing questions and require the engagement of the listener's imagination. In that regard, Donner's published sermons are noticeably different from those of Jan Bavinck, which were more consistently devotional and descriptive and did not make the same use of dialogical rhetoric.[10]

Bavinck was not wholly uncritical of Donner's preaching. For example, his comment on Donner's sermon in a journal entry on Sunday, October 18, 1874, remarks that while Donner's thoughts were "oh so beautiful," the sermon was let down by language and style that failed to match his content.[11] This critique is consistent with other accounts of Donner's preaching, which have described its strength as found in a combination of compelling biblical exegesis and a considerable knowledge of psychology, rather than eloquence or the possession of a pleasant voice.[12] It nonetheless remains clear that Donner's preaching and example inspired the young Bavinck and provoked a reaction within him. These years also saw him come under the influence of Abraham Kuyper, the rising star of a new wave of Dutch neo-Calvinism. Bavinck was introduced to Kuyper's Anti-Revolutionary Party (a Christian political movement directed against the anti-Christian influence of the French Revolution on Dutch society) by Donner, who would eventually become an Anti-Revolutionary Member of Parliament. At Leiden, Bavinck wrote a doctoral thesis on the ethics of the Swiss Reformer Ulrich Zwingli, following which he sought ordination in the Christian Reformed Church.

Leiden affected Bavinck as a preacher, as well as his thoughts on preaching and the formation of preachers. Apart from Bavinck's notes on Donner's sermons, the most revealing material on Bavinck the preacher from these years is found in his correspondence with Christiaan Snouck Hurgronje (1857–1936), a theologically liberal student who rose to prominence as an Islamicist, and with whom Bavinck maintained a close, lifelong friendship.[13] A letter to Snouck Hurgronje from August 3, 1878, describes the twenty-four-year-old Bavinck's reflections on his first experience of preparing and preaching a sermon:

> On Sunday, eight days ago in Enschede, I preached for the first time. I would have rather delayed it a bit, but my parents were enthusiastic and an aunt and uncle of mine, who live in Enschede, were invited specially. I had already promised them long before that I would preach my first sermon there, and because my aunt's health situation might well be that she doesn't have long to live, there was all the more reason to fulfil my promise. There was obviously much difficulty, and a lot of time lost before our exam. Writing a sermon was no small thing for me, but in the end it worked out. My text was 1 John 5:4b, "this is the victory that has overcome the world, our faith." I very much enjoyed preaching it. I was very calm and collected. Because of that, I am happy just to have done it, and the greatest difficulty

with [preaching] has already been conquered. However, I was still somehow unfulfilled, in that it had inspired me less than I had expected. I didn't speak with that feeling for myself as I had hoped and that I should; while the thought of always standing so far beneath the ideal was constantly with me. But overall it went well and I have an overabundance of reasons to be thankful.[14]

Further remarks from this period make plain that as a theology student, Bavinck struggled to prepare (and deliver) sermons well alongside his normal study routine. "I already see that preaching takes away an enormous amount of time. I have spoken once here and once in Zwolle. But I know that apart from once in Leiden, which I have promised to do, I will not think about preaching again before my doctoral studies."[15] Bavinck did begin to preach regularly toward the close of his Leiden years. By the end of 1879, he had preached thirty times and appears to have honed the skill of preaching without reliance on notes by speaking on the same two texts—1 John 5:4 and Galatians 2:20—on most of these occasions.[16]

The observation that the young Bavinck felt a certain experiential lack while preaching is particularly striking in view of the culture of experiential Reformed preaching within which he grew up. In 1881, reflecting on the personal challenge of studying at Leiden, Bavinck also remarked to Snouck Hurgronje that Leiden had deeply impacted his experience of preaching at that time:

> Their contemplations on Scripture aside, Kuenen and Scholten have not had much influence on me, if by that you mean losing my faith and taking on theirs. But they have indeed had (and it could be no other way) an influence on the power and manner with which I embrace those truths. That naïve and childlike faith, with its unlimited trust in the truth as it has been instilled, you see, has been lost; and that is a great deal; in that way their influence has been great and strong. Now I know that I can never regain that. That said, I find it good and am thankful for losing it. In that innocence there was much that was untrue and had to be purified. But still, there is that naïve (and I know no better word) something, that is good, that is a consolation; something that must remain if the truth is to stay sweet

and precious to us. Sometimes, very rarely (as where can you find the rock solid faith of yesteryear in our day and age?), I meet some people in my congregation who have just that, who fare so well by it and are so happy. Now, I can't help but wish that I believed as they did, so happy and joyous, and then I feel that if I were so, I could preach, animated, warm, always full of conviction about what I say; then I could be useful. I would be alive, living for others. But I know full well that this is in the past, it is no longer possible.[17]

In another letter to Snouck Hurgronje from the same period, Bavinck acknowledged that he was most aware of the personal, experiential cost of his years in Leiden while preparing to preach sermons.

Leiden has benefited me in many ways: I hope always to acknowledge that gratefully. But it has also greatly impoverished me, robbed me, not only of much ballast (for which I am happy), but also of much that I recently, especially when I had to write sermons, recognized as vital for my own spiritual life.[18]

An alternative rendering of this translation occupies a prominent place in Bolt's Editor's Introduction in each volume of the *Reformed Dogmatics*.[19] The English translation offered there is reliant upon Valentijn Hepp's 1921 work, *Dr Herman Bavinck*,[20] which quotes Bavinck's letter to Snouck Hurgronje (Jan. 13, 1881): "Maar het heeft me ook dikwerf zeer arm gemaakt . . . vooral als ik preeken maken moest."[21] In the Editor's Introduction, this is rendered as, "But it has also greatly impoverished me . . . especially when I preach." However, the translation of "als ik preeken maken moest" as "when I preach" (as a general statement made in the present tense) could be more accurately rendered as, "when I had to write sermons." (As will be explained, it refers to the sermons written in one particular period of Bavinck's young life.) In the Editor's Introduction to Bavinck's *Dogmatics*, the reader is introduced to a theologian jarred by his experience as an orthodox student in a liberal theological faculty. Immediately following the "especially when I preach" line, Bolt writes, "It is thus not unfair to characterize Bavinck as a man between two worlds."[22] The reader is left to wonder whether the act of preaching exposed the fault line between the two worlds Bavinck tried to straddle.

I have written at length elsewhere on the previously normative "two Bavincks" hermeneutic, whereby his works are read as the writings of two distinct persons pulled (and thus rendered irreconcilable) by the polar opposites of orthodoxy and modernity.[23] This approach, which normalized speech of the "modern Bavinck" and the "orthodox Bavinck," was highly unfruitful to Bavinck scholarship. It led to the creation of "orthodox" and "modern" groups among Bavinck's subsequent readership, each of which annexed certain portions of his work while rejecting others (on the grounds that those sections were written by "the other Bavinck"). It was founded on the assumption that Bavinck's thought contained no foundational concept that held together—even in great tension— things as diverse as modernity and orthodoxy. In *Trinity and Organism*, I argued for a new approach whereby Bavinck's doctrine of God enabled precisely this. For Bavinck, the Creator is the archetypal unity-in-diversity that enables and is revealed by the ectypal unities-in-diversity found throughout the creation. In that light, Bavinck's relationship to orthodoxy and modernity was recast. He was no longer a Jekyll-and-Hyde theologian, or "a man *between* two worlds." Rather, he was someone whose theological commitments enabled and required him to strive to be both orthodox and modern.

What does this debate on the "one" or the "two" Bavincks have to do with his preaching? Readers of Bavinck's *Dogmatics* may well be under the impression that he, one such "man between two worlds," found preaching difficult in a general ongoing sense, as though the act of preaching exposed Bavinck as a man straining between the pull of otherwise irreconcilable poles. Such an impression, however, must be refined somewhat. Beyond this early period, Bavinck's reflections on preaching present him as a man who found his task weighty and serious, but also existentially satisfying and a source of much joy.

In the letter in question, Bavinck referred to a specific instance of sermon preparation, rather than preaching in any general sense. The line "vooral als ik preeken maken moest" is most accurately translated, "especially when I had to prepare sermons." The sermons in question are helpfully noted by Harinck as those Bavinck had to write as part of his candidature for ordination in the Christian Reformed Church.[24] During this process, he had to preach a trial sermon on a preassigned text: "Let them alone, they are blind guides" (Matt. 15:14a). The text was chosen by F. J. Bulens with Bavinck's Leiden professors in view, with the expectation that Bavinck would prove his orthodoxy by openly distancing himself from them, subjecting them to explicit criticism as spiritually blind.[25] Bavinck's sermon did not conform to this prompting (a task he found personally difficult), but his candidature was nonetheless confirmed, and from that time on, he began to preach regularly. His choice of sermon texts in this period was strongly evangelical in character.[26] From then on, Bavinck came to find increasing joy in the act of preaching. Indeed, preaching (and pastoral ministry) played a central role in his own post-Leiden spiritual growth and the increasing sense of unity in his thought and purpose experienced in those years.

Soon after writing this letter, he became the pastor of the congregation in Franeker, a small town in the northern Dutch province of Friesland. The transition from a free student life to a busy pastorate was a shock to Bavinck:

> If you think for a moment, that I must preach twice every Sunday, teach the catechism four times through the week, must also devote much time to visiting homes and the sick, and then sometimes have to lead a Frisian funeral, you won't have to ask further whether any time or opportunity remains for my own study.[27]

Bavinck's diary gives his early impressions of preaching in Franeker. The entry dated March 20, the first Sunday following his induction (at which his father preached) reads: "Preached in Franeker on Isaiah 53:4–6 and Catechism Question 1 (completely improvised for the first time—it went well)."[28] This practice of preaching with no, or minimal, notes remained Bavinck's norm and explains why, despite his decades of preaching, only one of his sermons became available in print.

Although Bavinck was happy to serve in Franeker, his letters to Snouck Hurgronje make plain a range of challenges faced in his calling as a preacher. He found it difficult to cultivate his own Christian piety while having to mean so much to the spiritual lives of others, and lamented his singleness in the face of this.

> The most difficult part of my work is always to have to lift myself up to, and to stay at, the ideal level in my faith and confession. Oh, to have to deal with the holy constantly, always to be called to prayer, to thanksgiving, to exhortation or comforting. And then often to be able to project myself so little into those ever changing circumstances: that is hard, it creates a feeling of dissatisfaction and often of numbness. I now understand better than before how in the guise of the spiritual, a deeply unholy, unfeeling and insincere heart can reside. Apart from this serious and onerous difficulty in the office of the preacher, a shadow-side is attached, and I feel this deeply. And that is, that one is always "the minister," and can never more speak in a properly familiar way. That's how it is for me, anyway. Thus far, I haven't found anyone here with whom I can (or might dare to) enjoy that familiarity. And I find that difficult. At home I am alone, in my room, and outside I am always "the minister." If I ever longed for a wife who could understand me, and in whom I could confide fully, it is in these recent days.[29]

This sense of isolation was perhaps exacerbated by his own living situation: as he was a young unmarried minister, an older married couple went to live with him in the manse to take care of his domestic practicalities. Even at home, he was always "the minister" to others and had very little private space for relaxation. Despite these difficulties, Bavinck's brief stay in Franeker was appreciated by the congregation. Within a few months of his arrival, his own tone had become far more positive: "But I may not be thankless. So far it is going well for me, better than I had dared to think or expect. My preaching is not without fruit. I receive the congregation's love in abundance."[30] In a letter to Snouck Hurgronje in the following year, he recognized how little time for study he now had. In response to this, however, he wrote,

> I comfort myself with this, that I, in my role as a preacher do not work without blessing. When one of the old pious ones comes to me, who say to me how they were strengthened or comforted through my words, or others, who now know and lead a totally different life [than before]—that encourages me and gives me the impression that I haven't lived (and do not continue to live) on this earth in a wholly meaningless way. And such moments are priceless and could not be equalled by anything else.[31]

In 1882 he received (and declined) a call to a large Christian Reformed congregation in Amsterdam.[32] Later that year, Bavinck accepted a call to teach theology at Kampen, where he would remain from 1883 until 1901. Upon his departure from Franeker, one of the congregation's elders commented on the loss to "the whole congregation, and many beyond it," of its "very valued teacher," and "his glorious preaching."[33]

Bavinck's appointment at Kampen draws out a fascinating comparison with his father, who had received a call to teach there earlier in his life but had declined the appointment. Both were twenty-eight when faced with this decision. The significance of this circumstance was lost on neither man. Bavinck's diary entry (August 24, 1882) remarks on his appointment: "A striking moment for me and my father."[34]

Jan Bavinck's autobiography includes a remark by the Kampen professor Simon van Velzen that he enjoyed more influence among the Kampen faculty and students as a preacher than he might have found had he become a professor. Jan Bavinck's response suggests agreement with this observation:

> "Your influence on the students," Prof. van Velzen once said to me, "is still greater than that of the Professors." I shall allow this to be said by

the Professor, but this, I think, I might say, that both the Professors *and* the students have more than once declared to me that they were established through my preaching.[35]

Although Herman's years in Kampen are more closely associated with the production of his celebrated *Reformed Dogmatics*, the extent to which he also used his position there to influence and form his students as preachers should not be overlooked. This is most clearly seen in the booklet *Eloquence* (*De Welsprekendheid*),[36] published in the Kampen years. This text was intended as an extended theological reflection on the person of the preacher and the act of preaching itself, and offers fascinating insight into Bavinck's theologically rich engagement with both how *to preach* and how to *be* a preacher.

In 1891, he married Johanna Adrianna Schippers, who was ten years younger than Herman. Their only child, a daughter called Johanna Geziena, was born in 1894. His only published sermon was preached in the Burgwalkerk in Kampen in 1901. As has already been mentioned, Bavinck preferred to preach with no, or very minimal, notes, which goes some way in accounting for the lack of his extant written sermons. Why was this particular sermon noteworthy enough to end up in print? Bavinck himself points to the historic significance of its context in the introduction to the print edition:

> This sermon was preached on the occasion of President Kruger, with his retinue, being present in the gathering of the congregation during his visit to Kampen, on Sunday 30th June 1901. Many who heard it made known their desire that it should appear in published form. Although I could not literally give the sermon again, I have no objections to complying with this friendly request. The whole is now given concisely, in agreement with the words spoken on that day.[37]

Bavinck's sermon, titled "The World-Conquering Power of Faith," was attended by Stephanus Johannes Paulus Kruger (1825–1904), more commonly known as Paul Kruger, the president of the South

African Republic (Transvaal) and the face of Afrikaner resistance against the British during the Second Boer War (1899–1902). His text was 1 John 5:4b ("This is the victory that has overcome the world, our faith.") Also the text of his first-ever sermon, this verse functioned as a leitmotif in Bavinck's neo-Calvinism.

Viewed as a pair, *Eloquence* and "The World-Conquering Power of Faith" make for fascinating reading. In the former, we find Bavinck lecturing an audience of professors and seminarians. His grammar is sophisticated, he makes abundant use of foreign and ancient languages (assuming that his audience would need no translations), and he draws on material from the ancient world and high culture literature—all the while telling his students not to preach sermons as a demonstration of their own linguistic or cultural prowess. The latter text serves as a textbook example of the kind of preaching envisaged in *Eloquence*: it is exegetically focused and grammatically uncomplicated, it does not parade its preacher's learning, and its structure is clear and explained at the outset. It speaks as one moved soul seeking to affect another. These are texts that benefit from being read together.

During his time at Kampen, Bavinck was a key figure along with Kuyper in the 1892 Union of the Reformed Churches, which saw the Christian Reformed Church merge with a group led by Kuyper (the *Doleantie*) that had earlier seceded from the Dutch Reformed Church. A decade after this union, he accepted the post of theology professor at the Free University of Amsterdam (*Vrije Universiteit Amsterdam*).

This period in his life was marked by a broad and thorough engagement in the fields of politics (via the Anti-Revolutionary Party), philosophy, and education. In 1908, he gave the prestigious Stone Lectures at Princeton Theological Seminary in the United States. These lectures then appeared in print as the *Philosophy of Revelation*.[38] (His colleague Kuyper had also given the Stone Lectures in 1898, which became his *Lectures on Calvinism*).[39]

Although Bavinck continued to preach in these years, attention to this is perhaps crowded out by his heavy investment in other forms of public speaking. In that phase of life, Bavinck spoke regularly at all manner of public events: political rallies, youth assemblies, lecture committees, missionary organization meetings, university events, student gatherings, and so on. He, however, remained active as a preacher. While crossing the Atlantic en route to North America in 1908, for example, Bavinck shared the responsibility for providing onboard worship services with two fellow passengers (a German and an Englishman).[40] He preached eighteen times during this American journey.[41] As can be seen among this book's translated offerings, his efforts to understand and provide observations on American culture also included the distinct culture of the preaching he discovered there, and he paid particular attention to some of the most prominent preachers in North America at that time: the Presbyterians Joel Parker, Charles Henry Pankhurst, and Thomas De Witt Talmage all receive explicit (and critical) attention in Bavinck's explanation of American preaching to his own Dutch audience.

In 1920, after taking part in a synod in Leeuwarden, Bavinck suffered a heart attack. From then onward, his health began to fail. On July 29, 1921, within months of Kuyper's death, Bavinck died in Amsterdam, having preached for forty-two of his sixty-seven years.

BAVINCK'S FOREWORD TO *ELOQUENCE*

It has already been two years since this lecture on *Eloquence* was given in Kampen, on the 28th November 1889, for a public mostly composed of students from the Theological School. It was then published, but was only available for a short period and in limited numbers, and was never made available to purchase. From time to time, however, requests were made for the lecture to be reprinted and for it also to be made available to the general public. This is now being done. A few small changes have been introduced, but overall this second edition is the same as the first.

A new edition was deemed preferable, because the holy eloquence in question is in large part an undiscovered land in our Christian endeavors. Dutch pulpits are not presently overflowing with good, powerful speakers, never mind preachers. And this is all the more to regret, as the rich life that is currently unfolding outside the church obliges ministers of the gospel of Christ to apply themselves with all their might to developing the gift of the word. Indeed, with the public nature of life [in the present day], the meaning and influence of the word has increased in an exceptional way. While previously the pulpit was almost the only place from which the people could be reached, this is now replicated in all sorts of circumstances and lecterns, around which the public throngs. In the first place is the newspaper, whose printed word reaches the furthest parts of the society, in so doing exerting influence on the spirit and dominating public opinion. Following this, there are parliaments, political party days, meetings, conferences, gatherings of all sorts and for many goals, where the word is a mighty weapon that it never fails to do its work. In the present day there are more preachers outside, than inside, the church. Speakers, convinced and gifted speakers of all ranks and standings, are now found in all sorts of parties and movements. And they excite the people and draw them from the church to the auditorium. That this development in the life of the society is, in many regards, a cause for joy and thanksgiving does not need to be proved. But it is no less open to contradiction that it can be a grave danger for the flourishing of the church and the gathering of the congregation. When Spurgeon was battered in the press for his work in 1857, he responded in a sermon:

> In these days there is a growing hatred for the pulpit. The pulpit has maintained its ground full many a year, but partially by its becoming inefficient, it is losing its high position. Through a timid abuse of it, instead of a strong stiff use of the pulpit, the world has come to despise it; and now most certainly we are not a priest-ridden people one-half so much as we are a press-ridden people.[1]

It is wholly untrue, though, that the press alone does more than all these gatherings to detract from the church and from the word that it [the church] speaks. Many value attending many and all sorts of meetings as highly as or even more highly than regularly attending the public exercise of religion. No small number cherishes the thought that one can invest his time more usefully than by sitting for two hours in a church and listening to a sermon (that only repeats what one knows, or at least thinks he knows). Secularization thus advances broadly; solid knowledge of the truth is starting to become the exception [rather than the norm]; Bible and catechism are being exchanged for newspaper and magazine, for brochure and novel.

These new circumstances place a costly obligation on the church and call its ministers to an ever more faithful care for the office entrusted to them, especially in the ministry of the word. In content and form, the church's gatherings may not be inferior to the [secular] meetings that call to the people day and night. The church's gatherings are and, by virtue of their divine institution, must remain the center point of the religious life, the source of spiritual power, the inspiration for the work everyone is called to do, by the sweat of his brow, each weekday. Whatever influence there may be from the word in print or spoken that reaches us from elsewhere, it cannot be compared with the blessing there is for heart and life, family and society, in the word spoken to us in the gatherings of the congregation. Here alone do we find the ministry of God's word and the sealing of his covenant. Here, Christ himself lives in our midst and works by his Spirit. Here we taste the communion of saints, the forgiving of sins, and the principle of eternal life. The Sabbath is the best of days; no other day is like it. And the church is the meeting of God with his people; no other gathering can take its place or compensate for its loss.

Therefore, in our day as never before, the holy calling not to neglect the gifts entrusted to them rests upon ministers of the word, given to them for the declaration of the gospel. If they want to remain master of the people's conscience, they must ensure that they remain masters of the word. If, because of God's will, they may not passively watch as the stream of life passes by them and the church, they must first apply themselves to this: that the word of God in all its simplicity, truth, and power be commended to the consciences of men through their service.

Certainly, the gospel of Christ does not need our decorations, our energetic words of human wisdom; it is true and beautiful and rich in and of itself. But in order to present it in all of its glory, to speak it in a demonstration of the spirit and of power, constant practice, persistent effort, and loving dedication are demanded. Schleiermacher once rightly said,

> It is becoming, indeed, to apply the whole richness and magnificence of human discourse to the loftiest subject which language can reach— not as if there were any adornment, with which religion could not dispense, but because it would show a frivolous and unholy disposition in its heralds if they did not bring together the most copious resources within their power and consecrate them all to religion, so that they might thus perhaps exhibit it in its appropriate greatness and dignity.[2]

Paul has stated far more beautifully to the church at Corinth: "I am zealous for you with godly zeal. I promised you to one husband, to Christ, so that I might present you as a pure virgin to him."[3]

If the following lecture should serve to wake up this holy zeal somewhat, the writer's heart would be glad.

H. Bavinck
Kampen
May 1901

ELOQUENCE[1]

Permit me, in the time given, to request your attention for a lecture on eloquence. The choice of topic, it seems, needs no justification. I have the honor and privilege, in the first place, of addressing friends and brothers whose primary and only power shall later lie only in the word. The word, good sirs, shall be both your sword and shield, at once an instrument of attack and defense. Your might shall be greater, your influence wider, insofar as you handle that weapon with more skill. All other gifts pertaining to your spirits shall be more glorious to the extent that they are received by more powerful and enthusiastic expression. Servants of the Word, the Divine Word, shall be your honorable name. And with that, a power greater than that of monarchs and world leaders will be entrusted to you, because as master of the word, you are master of the conscience. He who rules the spirit is mightier than he who captures a city.

Although that high office of ministering the word is not suitable for many of my dear listeners, the hope may nonetheless be entertained that the subject of my lecture shall not appear unimportant. Speaking well is an adornment for each person, and for the Christian, man or woman, it is an exquisite virtue. More than we often think, the Holy Scripture places a strong accent on the dutiful, holy use of the tongue and of speech. Paul confronts each person without distinction, rather than an exceptional group, with the fundamental principle of all eloquence, when he says: "Let your speech always be gracious, seasoned with salt, so that you may know how you ought to answer each person."[2] Speaking well is not a requirement only in the pulpit or before the courtroom, but also in daily life and in social conduct. This general eloquence [*deze algemeene welsprekendheid*] is to be distinguished from verbosity [*welbespraaktheid*]. The particular instance of eloquence that I will discuss is simply a part and a narrower application of it. I remain convinced of your interest as I attempt to sketch this eloquence in its principle, essence, and form.

I. THE PRINCIPLE OF ELOQUENCE

You all remember the scene in Goethe's *Faust*, where he, translating John 1, can find no peace with the first verse: "in the beginning was the Word."[3] He does not like this expression at all. He cannot esteem the word so highly, he despises the word that is often, after all, so untrue; nothing but an idle sound or a hollow tone: the word cannot be the principle and origin of things. Accordingly, he wants to go further back, to descend more deeply; he wants to measure being, the root of things. So he writes: "in the beginning was the mind," which is thought, judgment, understanding. But that is written narrowly, for otherwise the doubt surfaces: Is it indeed the mind that works and creates everything? Is thought, just like that, indeed powerful enough to bring forth being? He improves his position once more and reads: "in the beginning was power." But once again he feels unsatisfied. This is also a position he cannot maintain; power on its own is also not yet capable of creation or generation, in the sense that it gives existence to a cosmos. He must go further back. There it comes to him and, comforted, he writes: "in the beginning was the *deed*." And with this new reading Goethe sets his pantheistic worldview in the place of the theism of the Holy Scriptures. For him, the beginning of the creature lies not in the living, self-aware, personal Word, which speaks to create all things. Rather, he seeks the principle and being of all things, as he says elsewhere, in restless activity [*Thätigkeit*]. There is a living, almighty will that penetrates all things, an "indefatigable interference," an eternal urge, which is also reason and love. He bears witness to this elsewhere in his poems:

In the infinite the same events
repeat themselves in eternal flux,
the thousand-fold vault of heaven
powerfully mingles with itself,
And joy of life streams from all things,
out of the smallest and largest stars,
and all urgency, all conflict
is eternal rest in God the Lord.[4]

The Holy Scriptures deny this naturalism directly and place at the beginning and as the principle of things not the unconscious power of the blind impulse, but the self-conscious, personal, independent word. Through wisdom, which God possessed as the beginning of his way, through the word as πρωτοτοχος της χτισεως, as firstborn of all creatures, God has called things which were not, into being, as though they were. By speaking, he creates and recreates all things. We wonder, and rightly so, at the mischievous beauty with which Homer describes the might of the greatest among the gods in the *Iliad*: "As he spoke the son of Saturn bowed his dark brows, and the ambrosial locks swayed on his immortal head, till vast Olympus reeled."[5] But what is this in majesty compared to the exalted words of the Scriptures: he speaks and it is so, he commands and it is done. Behold the absolute, divine, original power of the word. And all might from every other word springs from this and has therein its origin and image.

But as the word is the firstborn of all creatures, there is also a certain speech throughout God's creation. In all things there is thought, language, voice and sound and tone comprehensible to humanity. The creation is not simply a text written by the finger of God, and neither is it a silent book. More than that, it is a speech from God to humanity. I know well that we are often unable to decipher that book, with its hieroglyphic script, and that we are often unable to understand that speech. Poets, however, those wide-eyed children of the conscience, understand them and have appropriated that word from Paul: "There are many different voices in the world, and none is without voice."[6] The poet of Psalm 19 understood them;

"the heavens declare God's glory," he sings, "day to day pours out speech." In the whole creation there are no speech or words whose voice is not heard by all humankind. The speech of created things goes on until the end of the world. Everything speaks. Each thing has its own language and voice. The creation, in its entirety, is eloquent; sin is the only dissonance in its song.

As the human is the head of the creation, creaturely speech has reached its highest form in the human. All things show us God's footsteps, he [the human] is God's image, and not least so in his language. This very thing is a wonder. Its origin is unknown, its essence beyond searching out, its working indescribable. Bilderdijk[7] sang of this in verses well known to you:

> O, fluid sounds, in which, with breath poured out,
> the soul (as Godly light, in shafts sent out)
> itself shares! More than light or melody;
> Feeling's creation in closest harmony,
> Uniting incorporeal to matter, into convergence,
> Relieving the heart, which breathes and is glorified.[8]

The word seems to be idle, a trilling of air, a sound petering out on the breath of the wind, more idle than idleness itself. And yet [it is] a power mightier than sword or violence, as God's own word is both life and light. The word is not dead, it is no arbitrary symbol, no conventional sound, no idle work of art, sought "with difficulty and diligence" by active understanding. Rather, it is eager and living, cleansing, growing, degenerating, falling ill, and dying like every other organism. It is "created by feeling" and born of our very being, and not simply a product of the human will or a discovery by his brain. As the Word of God, the *Logos* is generated from his being and is not, as in Arianism, created by his will, so is it also with the word of the human. The word is the person himself, and language the soul of the nation. As such it adds more soul, more wisdom,

> Than Plato's School, than all of Athens together;
> Hold the Truth indeed, and true longing for heaven,

And include the treasures given us.
Know, O mortal, know your soul fully in her!
  She makes you human; your soul rests in her.
In speech perceive your own selfhood;
  And in so doing know yourself, and teach yourself to see God
    there![9]

In language you have the person, his being at its deepest and most intimate; in the word he steps into the light and appears from his hiddenness and reticence. This comes forth from the depths of his being. There, the affection that impacts us takes shape, and from the darkness of the birth canal the child of spirit and soul is born; a shadow, in turn, of man's glory and the express image of his inner independence. Language began, doubtless, in the same way, although we can propose nothing regarding the manner in which this took place. The first man, after all, was created as the image of God, and possessed therein not only righteousness and holiness, but also knowledge and truth. And what he knew of God and his works he had to represent in words. Thus was language born from his thinking soul, and that language was poetry. However,

The divine gift, with the breath of life
Descending upon the creature, as far as spirits hover,
(Is it also) with its fall, fallen and corrupted.[10]

And in this context this corruption exists herein, that the human, the same everywhere, is pleased to create, to give form, in words, free from the truth of thought. From content to form he is fallen, from being to appearance, from life to death, from light to darkness, from fullness to nothingness.[11] Then our word became empty and hollow, without life or light. It is against these idle, empty, emaciated words, against these χενοι λογοι [empty words], that the Holy Scripture so powerfully warns us, that we must give account for every idle word. Indeed, a considerable authority is exerted over us all in view of phraseology, hollow sounds, meaningless words, and conventional terms. Consider, for example, the dominion of the hollow sounds of "liberty," "equality," and "fraternity" that have been exerted upon and continue to dominate in the human heart. Whoever thinks himself able, trace the working that has proceeded in the previous two centuries from the slogan's immortality, virtue, tolerance, neutrality, equal rights for all, and so many more. These are all sounds that rustle in the ear, that caress the mind like the song of the Sirens, that bewitch the heart, but that offer no substance to one's thought. Upon deepening consideration they appear steadily emptier in meaning. But the pleasure regarding the vacuous form of the word is not restricted to these false slogans; all our conversation and almost all of our polite forms are strong proof of this. There is truth in Goethe's remark that "a man lies as soon as he becomes polite." Above Shakespeare's theater was the telling statement: *totus mundus agit histrionem*, "the whole world plays the actor." In *Hamlet*, Shakespeare sketches a man who considers the false and insincere existence of the world, who, therefore, trusts no one, and who finds a certain demonic desire to remove the masks of each person therein. As we also pay attention to the dark side of our human nature, it seems that Talleyrand[12] was certainly right to say: "Language was invented in order to conceal our thoughts."[13] We ought not to forget, however, that this sentence was written by a Frenchman and was intended for the French culture of his time. At that time, the French were the undoubted masters of conversation, which is to say, the art (as it is rightly named) of carrying out the most *gallant* conversations on the most *frivolous* subjects in the *finest* forms. No language was better suited to this than French. And no one was more deeply irritated by the shallow character of this language than the fine philologist Bilderdijk who voiced this belief in an all too passionate manner when he called out:

> Be gone! Thou bastard tongue. So base, so broken,
> By human jackals and hyenas spoken;
> Formed for a race of infidels and fit
> To laugh at truth and skepticize in wit;
> What stammering, sniveling sounds which scarcely dare

Bravely through nasal channels meet the ear,
Yet helped by apes' grimaces—and the devil,
Have ruled the world, and ruled the world for evil![14]

This preference for the form, for the tone, soon crosses over into lying, which is love for the opposite of being, for idle nothingness. Therefore, if to err is human, to lie is satanic. When Satan speaks, he speaks from within himself, which is to say, then is he true and upright. And the highest revelation of lying is false prophecy, the nihilistic opposite of the highest reality.

By paying attention to its opposite, its caricature, the real principle of true eloquence comes into its own! The root of idle words lies in the preference for the facade, in the human defection to the form and to nothingness. A person shall be eloquent, thus, if his word once again becomes the bearer of godly content, if it (in a creaturely sense) becomes what the *Logos* is in the divine being: both light and life. In order to speak *well*, one must exist *well*. Our word then becomes what it must be, as the image and likeness of ourselves, and we ourselves once again the image and likeness of God. Then it is not empty, idle, or hollow, but rather the revelation of the most intimate part of one's person, soul of one's soul, spirit of one's spirit. As with language, the source of true eloquence does not lie in the reasoning mind; indeed, it lies much less in an act or decision of the will, but rather lies behind both in his heart or spirit, from which life goes forth, also from the life of eloquence. If you compel the heart to speak, speak accordingly, and you will be eloquent. *Pectus est quod disertos facit* ("It is the heart that inspires eloquence"). *Les grandes pensées viennent du coeur* ("The great thoughts come from the heart"). All those who gave us their heart in their language were eloquent, those who in their words gave the best thing they had: namely, themselves.

Do not seek eloquence, therefore, in those "Sleepy John" types,[15] from those who sell tolerance and neutrality, those who do not know how to be hot or cold. They know no passion, no ardency, no enthusiasm or inspiration; they are not readily sought out by the

Muses of Eloquence.[16] Its secret lies in the soul. Let the heart's passion come to the word, and eloquence will be born. And what could not touch our hearts? Do we, along with the whole creation, not feel? Are we not connected to all things? Do we not belong at once to both heaven and earth? Our heart is the melting pot in which all things come together; it is the mirror whereupon all things are reflected. Impressions, perceptions, and emotions come at us from every side. We can be reached by the melodies of angels and the howl of demons, by creation's song and creature's sigh. There is no speech that cannot be understood by the human heart, no voice that cannot resound in our soul. And if our heart becomes so affected, so touched, or when our beautiful distraction is brought to the fore, and our heart is carried by it, and thus is awoken in passion, regardless of which one (love, hate, sorrow, compassion, indignation, shock, fear, angst, terror), if our conscience is touched and the waves of the life of the soul are set heaving, if our spirit is driven, and is set in motion and delight, then the real source of eloquence is unlocked within us. Deep, inner feeling is the principle of oratory; it is the soul's sensitivity to be jarred and aghast. Accordingly, poets and orators were always people of a fine and tender temperament, their natures finely attuned, by which the slightest touch was perceived, each chill causing the surface of their emotional lives to ripple. Not without good reason do we also read often that Jesus was moved by compassion. And when Paul held his mighty address on the Areopagus, his heart was moved by the observation that the city was so idolatrous. The same is true of all the orators from early and later times. The fury of Achilles, the faithfulness of Andromache, the patriotism of Demosthenes, the fervor of Cicero for the well-being of the city; all these are eloquent. The Reformers were eloquent, gripped by burning zeal for God's honor and finding expression in this regal word from Calvin: "A dog barks when his master is attacked; should I then not speak when my Master is assaulted?"[17] Burke was eloquent when he lifted up his mighty voice against the Revolution in the English Parliament. Multatuli[18] was eloquent in his *Max Havelaar*,[19] because his sense of indignation was provoked by the scandalous injustice of Droogstoppels and Slijmeringen[20] against the poor Javanese; eloquent in his own witness as the mother screamed in angst when her child fell into the water.[21] History supplies ample proofs that eloquence, as well as language, is a creation of feeling.

Second, the following is needed for the creation of true eloquence: a powerful emotional condition, a moved spirit, an affected heart, and an undeniable impulse to voice these feelings. These two are one. I have believed, and therefore I have spoken.[22] Whoever believes firmly and deeply cannot keep silent. Were he to do so, the stones themselves would call out.[23] This inspiration, vocation, internal impulse, this compulsion of the spirit, or however one should name it, is found in the highest sense in the prophets and apostles. Jeremiah says that it was in his heart as a burning fire locked in his bones.[24] Amos was a simple peasant, but he was so powerfully seized and driven that he could find no relief in his manual labor and left his flock behind. He could not ignore it; he had to go to Jerusalem to bear witness. And then he expresses this passion that consumed him inside: "The lion has roared, who should not fear? The Lord has spoken, who should not prophesy?"[25] And it is the same undeniable vocation that Paul pronounced in pain regarding himself, should he fail to proclaim the gospel. Yes, Jesus himself, in whom the Spirit dwells without measure, bears witness: "I have not spoken from myself, but the Father who has sent me, has given me a commandment, what I should say and I shall say."[26] This is the reality: *est Deus in nobis, agitante calescimus illio* ("there is a God within us who, when he stirs, sets us all aglow"),[27] the source of all higher life, of science and art, the principle also of true eloquence.

And immediately from this comes eloquence, without practice or preparation. There were orators in every people group, before there was rhetoric. Life precedes art. Homer stood at the inception of Greek culture and in one movement reached the greatest heights of poetry and eloquence. The apostles and prophets were eloquent, and that also without being rhetoricians. They had read neither Plato's *Gorgias* nor Cicero's *Oratory*; they had sought no schooling in Greek rhetoric. They did not know the works of Cicero and Quintilian, and the rules of discourse, for example, those of Schrant,[28] were totally foreign to them. They knew nothing of themes or divisions, of the analytic and synthetic methods, of peroration with sound effects, of discourse, all studied before the mirror. They knew nothing of any of these. They did not speak with impressive words of human wisdom, and yet they were eloquent and that on a higher level than the speakers in antiquity. They spoke in a demonstration of the spirit of power, as those with authority, and not as the scribes. They were eloquent, not by their own practice, but by divine gift; not by reflection but by inspiration; not by human calling, but by the power of divine right (*droit divin*). Eloquence for them was not design but nature, a gift rather than art. And still, now and then, confounding the rules, sometimes all at once and unexpectedly, from the dregs of the people there arise men whose word sets aflame the emotions of the people and strikes them like an electric shock. At the word of Peter of Amiens, the crusaders left for Jerusalem in their thousands. The mighty language of Luther reformed the shape of the whole of Christian Europe. In the seventeenth century, George Fox made the whole of England shudder by his prophetic speeches and his stirring voice. The [French] Revolution found its greatest herald and mightiest speaker in the rugged, irrefutable Mirabeau. And Multatuli's first work sent shockwaves through our own fatherland in its entirety.

But still, eloquence is not a single gift; it is also an art. It became that in the fatherland of all art and science, in Greece. There, it owed its origin to political freedom. In the people's assembly the word was the only way to victory and power. There were orators before there was rhetoric, but when the might of eloquence was noticed people spontaneously sought to explain it from its own essence, and thus its demands and rules were mapped out. Accordingly, the art of eloquence came into existence. It can never compensate for or replace talent. Rhetoric makes no one eloquent.

La vraie eloquence, Pascal said, *se moque de l'éloquence* ("The real eloquence mocks eloquence"). Art without talent is but the sophisticated hawking of words, fireworks without warmth; comparable to a soulless portrait but never a living picture. But talent without art all too often degenerates into coarse banality and annoying triviality, as the example of the popular orators shows. Talent, which art despises, is also not the true talent. Which talent that comes from above and recognizes its dependence should be able to scorn the means also given from above that continue its development? The notion that genius has nothing to do with work and diligence, and must rather patiently wait for inspiration, is wholly wrong. The idea of F. A. Wolf, "*Genie ist Fleiss*" ("genius is diligence"), is exaggerated; no less one-sided is the notion that divine gifts make all human effort and practice superfluous. Rückert[29] is far closer to the truth when he says:

> This is a true saying: the artist is born
> But every truth becomes error in the mouth of fools.
> [An artist] is born with an artistic impulse, but not the art itself
> Formation is his work, the talent is [due to] heavenly favor.[30]

Men great in art and science have thus never reached the highest peaks of acclaim without the most careful practice and the most persistent effort in all their powers. The orators whose names are passed down from generation to generation, such as Demosthenes and Cicero, spared themselves no effort in developing and perfecting their latent talents. And thus it is so: the art is undergirded by the gift, and the latter is the first and most important; and yet, also regarding the word of the Bible, the gift may not be overlooked in any area. The gift demands and calls for the art.[31] Talent may not be able to bring forth and feed the stream of eloquence, but can lead it into a pleasant river. But whatever true eloquence is, talent or art or both together,[32] it finds its source only in the human heart. Herein lie its origins. "From the overflow of the heart speaks the mouth."[33] Rightly has eloquence been named *la raison passionnée* ("passionate reason").

II. THE ESSENCE OF ELOQUENCE

As such, the principle of eloquence is known to us. However, what is eloquence in itself, and in what does its essence consist? I fear no objection should I describe it as the gift developed by the art, by the power of the word to convince the mind, touching the conscience and persuasively affecting the will of the people. All eloquence, where also appropriate, in daily life, whether in the pulpit or in the council chamber, is actually threefold: argument, description, and persuasion. The eloquent person must know what he has to say, possess a solid knowledge thereof, and convincingly persuade the understanding of his hearers; this points us to the connection between eloquence and philosophy or science. Further, he must not only present an argument; he must also provide description and with this touch the conscience of the people. This shows the coherence that exists between eloquence and poetry. Finally, he must persuade and move the hearers' will. This shows us the connection between eloquence and virtue. None of these three can be missed. The word that must go out in order to be eloquent must come from the whole person, it must bear his image and likeness, it must also be directed to the whole person, to understanding, heart and will. Only in this manner does it arrive at its destination which in our case is always, albeit in a creaturely way, no different from that of the Lord our God, who creates and recreates all things in his own image by his word.

1. Eloquence thus first demands a sound knowledge of the matter about which one is speaking. The Sophists, the men of the Enlightenment (*Aufklärung*), and the phraseology of Socrates' day made eloquence into a form of trickery, a dexterity, that applied itself to oratorical words, bombastic sentences, stunning pictures, clever puns, striking antitheses, and that therefore surprised the conscience of the people. Gorgias, in Plato's work of the same name, makes no secret of it. A rhetorician is someone who without study and through his word pageantry alone can speak more beautifully and ravishingly than the real experts on any given subject:

on politics with politicians, on medicine with the doctor, on war with the warrior; and *he* exceeds and conquers everyone in popular gatherings by his dazzling talents as an orator. Their highest art was thus: τον ηττω λογον χρειττω ποιειν, which is, to speak in black and white. To work an effect, the achievement of success, was the goal of their strivings. Socrates and Plato waged war against this and declared this sort of eloquence to be a part of the art of flattery, χολαχευτιχη, and set it alongside gastronomy, οφοποιιχη, which also has no higher goal than to caress the desires and excite the sense of taste. And in place of this they demanded solid philosophical knowledge of the orator. Socrates said that the orator must not overcome the hearer by the splendor of his words, but rather must convince by evidence, and also that he must not chase momentary success. He must place himself in the service of God; he must throw himself into the breach for morality and justice. Plato described true eloquence as a leading of souls by the word, ψυχαγωγια τις δια λογων, and deemed this only possible when the orator possessed knowledge of the philosophy of the highest ideas, which can only captivate and excite the human soul by virtue of its divine origin.

In spite of this mighty objection, however, the generation of the Sophists did not die out in the time of the orators. They live among us into the present day. There remain numerous people, who, according to Fénélon,[34] speak not because they have something to say, but to look for something to say, because they must speak. Schopenhauer[35] divides writers in three classes: first, those who write without thinking—this class, he says, is the most numerous. Then there are those who think while writing. These are also great in number. Finally, there are those who already have thoughts, and then set about writing: these are extremely rare. This division can be applied to public speakers in exactly the same form. Those whose public speech takes place in the pulpit are no exception to this. There is perhaps nowhere else that the phrase occupies a mightier and more significant place than here. Pompous voice, blaring speech, drawn out tone, empty sentences, and flattering terms must compensate for what is lacking in sound content and real study. This is all the more remarkable here because the servant has God's Word to declare, and this conviction must forbid him in the strongest terms from putting anything in the mouth of Holy Scripture than what it actually says. The text, however, is often just a hook, upon which the tattered rags of one's own or the people's favorite meanings are hung. Allegory, spiritualizing, mystical meaning, deeper meaning, a truth behind the truth, is thus the process by which one's own thoughts are reconciled with Scripture. Study is not necessary for this. One needs only creative dexterity, an unfettered sense of fantasy, a considerable dose of insolence, and a conscience not given to pressing on these things.

These preachers do find success, more so than the Sophists. When they are asked, "Why did Moses catch the snake by its tail, and not by the head?" they dare to answer profoundly: "Because its head was crushed in paradise." With a mystical glance they perceive the five books of Moses in the five husbands of the Samaritan woman. In the wedding of Isaac and Rebecca they see foreshadowed the manner wherein Christ won his bride, the church. When one dares to declare all of this, and much more, as God's word, there will be no shortage of success. But the servant of the gospel then makes true the cynical but also spiritual parody given by Multatuli in the stirring sermon of the Honorable Rev. Zielknyper.[36]

To counter this and similar phraseology as much in the boardroom and courtroom as in the pulpit, there is but *one* effective medicine: hard study, solid knowledge, and real science. Sincere piety does not mean that one is sufficiently on one's guard against this. This kind of preacher is not always devoid of heartfelt piety. But such study teaches us what we may declare in God's name as His thoughts. The preacher of the gospel must say after Jesus, in his way: "I have not spoken from myself, but the Father who has sent me, has given me a commandment, what I should say and I shall say."[37] This alone gives that respect, the need for which is unmistakable, for eloquence in the pulpit. Without this respect this eloquence would never have arisen and could not remain in existence. To the extent that we lose the conviction of the Divinity of the Word that we bring, our preaching loses influence and power. Should we have no Divine message to bring, who gives us the right to stand before people from the same contexts as us, who are perhaps better than us? Who then gives us freedom to elevate ourselves above them in the pulpit, to busy them on the most important matters of the soul and of life, and even to declare to them an eternal "yes" or an eternal "woe"? Who dares this, who may do this, but those who feel themselves called by the Lord? Such can only be eloquent. That is the unmissable, but also the incomparable might of the preaching of the word. But with this one should also know that what one declares is not our own, but is rather God's word. Therefore it is also irresponsible and fundamentally unbelief to use the word of God in order simply to declare opinions which please the people. This eloquence, however orthodox it might sound, is a part of χολαχευτιχη, flattery, which Plato set alongside gastronomy in one line.

However, if virtuous knowledge is the first element of true eloquence, one must not fall into the other extreme and make the oratorical speech an arsenal of learning. The pulpit is not a lectern, and the church is not a school. However, this side is also often sinned against. Our Reformed fathers often plundered the treasures of Hellas and Latium and laid them out before the congregation. Hebrew, Greek, and Latin, sometimes even Syrian and Arabic, geography, history, and archaeology had to be brought into service, in order to fill the whole church with amazement at the learnedness of their minister. Rev. Eversdijk has left us a strong, clear example in his sermons on the glory of the Messiah:

> We read there that a friend is full of spiritual fondness for his friend, as he is to himself. In Deut. 13:6 we read that he is like our own soul. A friend is therefore expressed as an alter ego, another I. So was Lycrius, in praying for his friend: *Serves animae dimidium meae*, save the other half of my soul. The proverb is, by the way: *amicus una est anima in duobus corporibus*. Friends have one soul in two bodies. Laërtius tells that Xenocrates adored Plato with such a great love that when Dionysius said to Plato, "*caput tibi quisquam tollet*," someone—with all his might—shall take off your head, standing there, [he replied]:

"*nullus id prius, quam istud abscindet,*" no-one shall cut it off soon. See, such a friend is the Messiah.[38]

Well now, that is not preaching or eloquence. It is trivial flaunting of learnedness and idle parading of words! Solid knowledge includes, rather than excludes, simplicity. Learnedness is not wisdom. Beets[39] rightly says: "He who seeks knowledge but not wisdom thereby, sleeps with the chambermaid and bids the wife goodbye."[40] Preaching learnedly, so that the people [do not], and so that not even you yourself, understand, is not an art. But just as in Holy Scripture, the highest ideal in solid preaching is to speak out the deepest thoughts so simply and so naturally that even the casual laborer understands you. In this context Luther once said during his table talk: "I preach for the unlearned and commend to all. If then I know some Greek and Hebrew, I keep that to myself, until we are in learned company. Thus we sometimes make it so varied that our dear Lord wonders at it."[41]

2. Knowledge, however, is insufficient for the orator. The philosopher demonstrates and convinces, and is directed only toward the understanding. But the orator does not simply demonstrate, he does not only narrate; he offers. He also focuses on the conscience and the imagination. Eloquence is therefore closely related to poetry. The art of poetry was the mother of eloquence. Homer was the father of both poetry and the history of eloquence. Demosthenes observed his art and was molded by his example. Particularly in the East, oratory and poetry went hand in hand. The prophets of the Old Covenant were orators and also poets; the harmonious rhythm of their language continues to prove this. The comparisons of Jesus unite both in himself. And 1 Cor. 13 is a moment of eloquence from Paul, while also being a song, a hymn on love. But slowly, eloquence and poetry were separated. Eloquence became independent and has become increasingly estranged from poetry. For Western people, the understanding speaks more strongly than the imagination. We live in the abstract, rather than the concrete. Reflection rules over intuition. We long for "more truth than beauty,

more healthy understanding than glorious words, more wisdom than adornment." We are increasingly distant from the age of popular poetry. Even the naivety of the Middle Ages has passed us by, never to return.

And yet, eloquence and poetry remain connected. They are of the *same* family. They are in each other's blood. And this relatedness pronounces itself in the picture common to both: in the vitality and clarity of the presentation, in the use of image and figure, in their common gift, *"de faire voir les objects"* ["to demonstrate objects"]. The orator must make us perceive what he is saying. The address is an argument, but it is also a drama, a spectacle. It describes what sin is, for example, not only in dogmatic terms. It also lets us see it in its awful guilt, in its devastating power. It does not simply lay out the various sins in dogmatic form. Rather, it performs them, not, obviously, by imitation, but by animated presentation: the drunkard, the miser, the servant of the world, the impure of heart. It offers no philosophical handling of virtue and religion. Rather, it performs them in a living body before our eyes.

The preacher of the gospel should be able to do this better, because everything in Christianity is concrete, clear, and personal, or if you wish for the deepest ground [for this], because it is Trinitarian.[42] In this regard the servant of the word has a huge advantage over all other speakers in the civil, legal, and social worlds. It is always the case that if he does not stay on the surface of things, but dares to descend into the deep, he finds himself standing face to face with a person, in creation, in salvation, in sanctification. The Holy Scriptures are also therefore a mighty history, from beginning to end. They never give abstract reasoning or dogmatic argumentation. There is never the language of reflection on the word. They do not argue; they paint a picture. They do not describe; they narrate. They do not prove; they show. In this regard there is no other book in this world to compare to the Scriptures. Everything therein is clear, artistic, concrete, original, as fresh as crystal-clear water that bubbles from its source. Scripture speaks in the language of life, of the heart, of immediacy, of inspiration, and is thus understandable for every man, going forth into every generation, never growing old in its time, and therefore classic in the highest sense, in an utterly unique sense of the word. In Scripture, divine thoughts are woven into history; prophecy and history are *one*. In its entirety, from start to finish, it is thought given flesh, the incarnate Word, divine anthropomorphizing, the spiritual placing of everything in wide circles orbiting around him,[43] in whom the Godhead dwells in bodily form, and in whom the ideal becomes reality. The abstract dualism of God and man, spirit and matter, heaven and earth, the mind and the heart, is here reconciled in the most intimate oneness.

In order to fulfill the two demands of eloquence, therefore, there is no better study than that of the Holy Scriptures. In this regard, every sermon loses clarity as it lets go of the historic Christianity of the Scriptures. See this, for example, in the miserable Rationalism of earlier and later times. Try, if you will, to transpose the Semitic into the Japhetic;[44] try to remove the divine idea from history. But [in so doing] you have not only deprived Christianity of its marrow and core, you have also deprived religion of its poetry. Recent attempts to join poetry and religion anew, to breathe new life into the withered concepts of understanding, have been in vain. Even the call for help to imagination, song, and art does not enrich this poverty. Rationalism is the death of poetry. It makes everything, even language, abstract. God becomes the Supreme Being, the Messiah becomes the sage from Nazareth, reconciliation becomes example, sin becomes a shortage, conversion becomes self-betterment. All symbolic, illustrative words make way for arid concepts. While true eloquence illustrates thought, Rationalism dissolves the clarity of history into cold mental images. Therefore, Rationalism and eloquence fight with each other just as fiercely as do Rationalism and poetry; true eloquence is illustration. In her hands, the abstract begins to live, and moves from thought into flesh and blood. When, for example, the famous Bernard of Clairvaux wishes to declare the saving decree to the people, he sets forth four divine attributes: mercy, truth, peace, and wisdom speak and act for us. Such eloquence cannot but excite and fix the people on the lips of the preacher. Born of feeling, it [eloquence] makes itself known in the language of imagination. And imagination, according to Bilderdijk's beautiful image, is the womb of poetry, but it must be fertilized by feeling. And from this, for both eloquence and poetry, is "a new universe born,"

> Where borne on wings of his power,
> Whirling and floating with Godly fulfilment,
> Poetry calls shining worlds out of their graves.[45]

Obviously, however, one can go too far to the right on this. There is sometimes overkill, *das Guten zuviel*, on this side. The connection between eloquence and poetry certainly does not mean that one's sermons must rhyme. In the past—certainly among ministers, though I do not know about the people—this was in fashion. Rev. Antoine Croezen began the sermon at the inauguration of the Nieuwe Kerk in Rotterdam in 1737 with the call to worship in poetic meter:

> Bless us Father and Son
> Bless us Holy Ghost
> Show honor, everyone
> For Him you fear the most.[46]

Another crossed over to his text with this verse:

> Most lovely Jesu,' we are here
> You and your word to obey;
> Our words thus so steer,
> That its power go not astray,
> May rather our hearts know mirth,
> Enraptured by your worth! Amen.[47]

Still more foolish was a catechist, who let his poetic tendency flow out in these words during an oration on the pious Rev. Velingius:

> Piety paused and gave a kiss
> In honor to Velingius.[48]

But more prosaic preachers have also failed to rein in their imaginations in this regard. It is too artificial when Rev. Mees entitles a sermon on Sarah's burial as, "The stately mourning burial of the blessed princess Sarah, deceased housewife of the outstanding prince, prophet, and friend of God, Abraham. Buried for 3,539 years at Hebron, in Makpela, in the year 2145 post-creation, 1858 years before the birth of Christ, after living 127 years, and her husband, 138 years." Neither will it please us when Rev. Zelotes of Rotterdam announces his text as follows: "The words of our text were created from the great ocean of Moses, the fourth fountain, the fifteenth vessel, the twelfth drop."[49] And even less can we give our approval to Rev. Theod. à Brenck's realistic picture: "When water has flowed into a ship, it is thrown out again in a bucket. In this way, David, through the bucket of upright confession, threw out the water of sin in the ship that was his soul, which had entered through the cracks of breaking God's commandments." In the past, such bad taste was enjoyed. That was the time of the famous poet Jan Vos,[50] who writes of a love-struck youth speaking to his heart's chosen one:

> I let the scepter slip,
> If I with my mouth on the shores of your lips,
> May be stranded with a kiss.

I dare not assert that the people of today would no longer find such false ingenuity charming. Affected and vulgar speakers have always excited the majority of people. The naturalism and realism of Zola[51] falls into the territory of religion in the taste of many. But there is *one* thing to be learned from these popular speakers: the artistic, the lively, the graphic quality of their performance. This is perhaps the secret of all popular eloquence: the speaker may not isolate himself from his listeners, not even for a single moment, and may never hold a cold monologue. To the contrary, he must constantly turn to his hearers, see them, appeal to them, pose questions, set objections in their mouths, clear away resistance. He cannot leave them to themselves for a single second, he must keep them occupied and involve himself in this; he must speak to them and deal with them. There must be exchange, intercourse, business done from eye to eye, hand to hand, and soul to soul. The speech must be a single dramatic act. Eloquence is the first to reach this goal, for which Bilderdijk also reprimands the poets:

> Hold all hearts in your hands!
> Burrowing, rooting in our bowels!
> Master imagination and understanding!
> Knead, knead our mind with your fingers!
> Learn from Jupiter to throw lightning!
> And so set souls ablaze!
> The common folk may to the heavens
> Staring at you, try to follow
> the feeling in your shocked heart!
> The sorrow and laughter, the glow and the shiver
> To which your song's tone falls or rises,
> Or sinks in immovable despair.
> Hate and love make themselves open,
> Binding [the people] to the punishment
> Induced, brought by your hand.
> And have feeling, neither will nor life,
> Only what your song's tone is able to give,
> As you drag it through the waves.[52]

3. However intimate the connection between eloquence and poetry is, and to the extent that they go together, eloquence is nonetheless higher than poetry. Eloquence has to reach a direct and immediate goal, and must place in our consciences the same affections felt by the poet. That said, eloquence does not appeal only to our intellect. It does not stir and shock only the conscience. It is unsatisfied with affection in our souls. The final goal of preaching does not consist of—to borrow a clichéd expression—flooding God's house with tears. Soul-stirring and tear-jerking preachers—as Witsius[53] called them—are not always the best. Beets' words are apt for such evocative preaching:

Jan War's sermons are stirring, say you,
Come! I want to believe it too.
His words alone can stir a pot through,
From top to bottom turning the stew.[54]

True eloquence aims at more than stirring the conscience. It tries to go through the intellect and heart in order to move the will of the person. The orator may not be satisfied until his hearers think, feel, and act as he does. In eloquence the word first reaches its highest, reforming, recreating power; it approaches the original, absolute might of the word of our God most closely.

> Real eloquence is, therefore, inconceivable without mastery of language. Prof. De Vries, upon his admission to a professorship in Groningen in 1849, pointed to this as a crucial demand and hallmark of eloquence. He described this mastery in these words: If the speaker has so internalized the content of the language that they are almost united in being, if the language itself has so become his possession in its matter and spirit that all its treasures are available to him on cue; if every thought that arises within him, and every sensation that he feels, causes the best word and expression with which it can be vividly portrayed to spring to mind immediately; if agreement and connection, the curve and fold of the parts, the exchange of form and turns, which seals the absolute finest gradation and the purest agreement, which merges into one tone with the trilling of feeling's every sinew; and finally, if each image picked up by the soul from the mirror of language, equally powerful, equally clear, was reflected with the early haze of originality in the living word; then has victory been won. Then language has found its master.

This mastery over language assures us first of dominion over the conscience and, as such, over the will of the people. This will is no mere weather vane turning in the wind. Rather, its being is rooted deep in human nature. The preacher of the gospel must therefore *implore* his hearers that they be reconciled to God.[55] Eloquence is a plea, a drama, and an act; and finally, it is more than all of those things together: it is a fight and a struggle. The orator must wrestle with his hearers. He must persuade them. He may not give up on this fight until they have given themselves over. He must clear away all opposition, strip them of every excuse, and cut away every escape route. He must drive them into the narrow space where they, like the Israelites, could move neither forward nor backward, neither left nor right; they could only look above, from where their help should come.

The great seriousness, the heavy responsibility of the ministry of the word, makes itself clear in its task of persuasion, and that more strongly than in its argumentation and illustration. But precisely from the standpoint of the Reformed confession is this responsibility, heavy as it may be, bearable. If conversion were dependent on the will of man, and if the will could occupy itself with this to its heart's content, then the preaching of the gospel would be a task too burdensome for a man. Each sermon that did not bend the will of its hearers would be an irrefutable witness against you, against your effort and diligence, and as such an unbearable self-reproach. With yet more powerful words, and with more serious effort, the human will could have been bent by your eloquence. But as this is not so, and as dominion over the will remains with the Spirit of God, the persuasive demand of eloquence is something that can be taken on one's shoulders: the preaching of the word is accompanied by the work of the Spirit, and the word of the minister is simply the means in His almighty hand.

Regarding this practical and ethical goal, many have set up eloquence in an intimate connection with good and virtue. Cicero claimed, as has been repeated by Quintilianus, that the orator, to be a true orator, must be a virtuous person.[56] Socrates demanded that the rhetorician should place himself in service of God, and should only use his gifts for the defense of justice and morality. In our time, the famous orator Theremin[57] could assert that eloquence was a virtue and rhetoric a section of ethics. This is without doubt excessive. Eloquence is a gift, and one that is also found in those who use it in the service of sin. Mirabeau, Heinrich Heine,[58] and Multatuli serve as ample proof of this. And yet, Theremin's assertion contains a profound truth: the connection between eloquence and virtue is natural, whereas that between eloquence and sin is unnatural and is always created artificially. The beautiful is the normal, only, and natural clothing of the true. Lies and sin can steal that robe of truth and holiness, and dress themselves up as angels of light, but the truth is elegant by nature. It is beautiful by virtue of its simplicity; it needs no gaudy jewelry. Lies, however, being in and of themselves poor, are forced to wrap themselves up in the garment of truth and, as such, to pay tribute to it. Naked, they please Satan alone but do not please any single human. No one loves lies of his own accord. There have doubtless been those who preached errors. False prophecy has always had mighty oratorical talents at its disposal. Rousseau's *The Creed of a Priest from Savoy* [*profession de foi du vicaiare Savoyard*][59] is full of beauty. Mirabeau's eloquence was overwhelming. Recall only that powerful word with which he answered the king's request to disperse the people's gathering: "Go and tell your master that we are here by the power of the people, and that we will only be removed by the power of the bayonet." [*Allez dire à votre maître, que nous sommes ici par la puissance du peuple, et qu'on ne nous en arrachera que par la puissance des bajonettes.*] Lammenais' *Words of a Believer* [*Paroles d'un croyant*][60] is a Revolution hymn in a biblical style. None of these in any way invested their gifts in the service of God, as the heathen Socrates demanded, but they were nonetheless eloquent and could only be so through the elements of truth they defended, and above all, through the firm sense of belief by which they embraced lies as truth. Without this sense of belief, human eloquence remains impossible. And thus, eloquence can only reach its highest triumph when it is free and, according to its own nature, stands in service of truth and holiness. In that way it has often been powerful, not only enlightening the mind and jolting the conscience, but also bending the will of thousands, renewing society, saving the city, and changing the face of nations. In the word there is an unbelievable, almost Divine power. Think of Demosthenes to Phillip, of Cicero to Catilina, of Napoleon at the foot of the pyramids. Think of Lamartine who tamed the furious mob by the power of his word on the steps of the City Hall in Paris in 1848. Or do you wish for an example of eloquence in the pulpit? Recall then the sermons of Massillon[61] in 1701, held during Lent for Louis XIV and his royal court. Bring to mind this poignant section of the sermon on the "few who are chosen":[62]

> Therefore I fix my thoughts on you, brothers, who are gathered here. I do not speak of other people; I consider you alone as worthy. See which thought occupies me and compels me hesitantly. I ask you to imagine that your last hour has passed and that the end of the world has arrived: that the heavens will open above you, while Jesus Christ appears in full glory in the middle of his temple, and that you have gathered here with no goal but to wait for him, and while you tremble as evildoers, for whom either grace or condemnation to eternal death shall be declared. . . .
>
> Now then, I ask you, and while I direct this question to you, I shudder with angst because at this moment I do not want my lot to be parted from yours and I feel myself so disposed, as I wish you would be. I ask you then: If Jesus Christ, who is most majestic in all the universe, should appear in his temple, in the midst of our meeting, to make that terrible division between the sheep and the goats, do you believe that the majority of those gathered here would be on his right-hand side? Do you not believe that the difference between the two sides would be great? Do you believe that the Lord could find ten righteous ones here, whom he could not find in five entire cities? I ask you, you do not know, and neither do I. You alone, O God, know who belongs to you. But if we do not know who is his, we know at least that sinners do not belong to him. Very well, who is gathered here? I do not count titles or honors; in the presence of Jesus Christ they are of no avail. Who are you? Many of you belong with sinners, who do not want to be converted; a greater number belong with those who would want to be converted, but who are putting that off; many are barely converted and then fall back into sin; a great number believe themselves to need no conversion: what a lineup of the damned! Remove these four kinds from the holy gathering, who shall quickly be removed on the Day of Judgment: And now appear, you pious ones; where are you? The Elect of Israel, go to my right hand! You who belong to the

good wheat, be separated from the chaff, which shall be thrown in the fire. O my God, where are your chosen ones, and what remains of your possession?

The impression made by these words was exceptional. The king and all who surrounded him, the whole company, shuddered. The preacher, who was also dumbfounded by the general emotion, was silent for a moment, and covered his face with his hands.

III. THE FORM OF ELOQUENCE

Finally, I request another moment of your attention to the form of eloquence. This is doubtless secondary to the content and matter. Eloquence follows a different rule than poetry. In poetry, the form is of equal importance to the content. Its goal is to please. In poetry, beauty seeks immediate incarnation. In eloquence, the form, language, and presentation are wholly subject to the content. Having already defined the content of eloquence, I now take the liberty to think of its presentation. We may not value the presentation as highly as Demosthenes and des Amorie van der Hoeven,[63] who considered it the first, second, and third, the be all and end all, of eloquence. And yet, it is surely of great and more than secondary worth. Many public speakers not lacking in natural gifts undervalue it sorely in its power and meaning. In comparison to it, an indefensible nonchalance often dominates. Certainly, speech like that of the aforementioned des Amorie van der Hoeven is only for a small number of "chosen ones." Placing the form as the ideal, for which every public speaker had to strive, undervalued the diversity of [speakers'] gifts, and for the majority served as a path toward disappointment and discouragement.

This much, however, can be demanded of each one who speaks in public, that he fight an earnest fight against all the unnatural mannerisms that disfigure the speech of so many. Here, I do not refer at all in the first place to the manner of preaching, for the salvation of which de Génestet[64] prayed. The modern, profane

manner set in its place by many is no more suitable for the high
and earnest content of the gospel of the cross. But there are other
unmannerly things, not only found among preachers but rather
among all kinds of speakers, which must be warred against. An
amusing list of these affectations could be made up, that speakers of all kinds have made their own. There is a written sermon
given in 1500 in Bruge by Olivier Maillard that contains "Hmm!
Hmm!" throughout, where he, in following the solemn norms of
that time, had to clear his throat. The most wondrous vocal sounds
and the strangest postures are often saved for the public pulpit.
No intonation so bizarre is heard but from the pulpit, and no ges-
turing so ridiculous as that seen behind the lectern. With many
speakers, it is as though they are turned into new people, "*orators*,"
when dressed in jacket, formal dress, or academic gown. Their
voices taken on an abnormal tone and start reverberating, howl-
ing, screaming, and shrieking; their faces contort into the most
unnatural creases; their eyes roll; they make fists; their hands wave,
strike, hammer, and turn like the wings of a windmill; their feet
dance, jump, and stamp; some speakers do not spare their hearers
their even less attractive nasal and guttural sounds. This is wholly
against Beets' beautiful lesson:

> Let beautiful verses from plain lips smoothly flow,
> But not fierce and loud shriek or peal or boom or bellow.
> From hammering, waving and rowing, curb hand and arm,
> Acting the windmill brings no charm.[65]

These are attributes and idiosyncrasies that in no way pertain only
to preachers, and which can be found just as strongly in other
speakers. If they seem to be found mostly among the teachers of
the church, it should be noted that these form by far the greatest
number of public speakers. But it is also true that the best, and the
majority of good, speakers are to be found among them. Regarding
eloquence, ministers, for all that they are ridiculed and lambasted,
can hold their own very well among other orators. They can also
offer excuses that other speakers cannot. In the first place, they are

called to speak before the same audience two, three, or more times
a week; and whoever does not know this from [his own] experience
has very little idea how much effort that requires, and while doing
so, to stay always on guard against all these unnatural mannerisms.
In addition to this, they must also often speak in rooms where
the building design laughs at the laws of acoustics and which cor-
respond to what seems the only law of Reformed church building
style: "as many bodies as possible in the most ominous room possible."[66] And finally, thanks to our conservatism, preachers of the
gospel always have to carry out their task in those narrow, closed,
elevated pulpits that in no small way have advanced a stiff, unnatural, artificially holy kind of eloquence, and that have killed the
simplicity, togetherness, and liveliness of preaching. This was such
that de Génestet, a child of his time sitting under the pulpit, could
utter the touching complaint:

> You preacher high above to see,
> Have you there no word for me?
> Your sermon like an echoing fiat,
> Rolls along empty past my spirit.[67]

But whatever excuses can be offered, they never dismiss the demand to invest all our care not only in the content of eloquence
but also in its form, which is to say, in speaking. For this it is un-
necessary, and even less is it good, that we all conform ourselves
to *one* model. The diversity of individuals comes into its own in
public speaking. Each has his own, and each has therefore but *one*
[kind of] speech. That of the others is, for him, a caricature. But
we are not born with this single [kind of] speech ready-made (*fix
und fertig*). We are not born fully fitted in any way, or for any task.
Life is no idyllic rest; rather, it is a serious struggle. The single good
and fitting speech that we bring with us, and that only in seed form
and ability, is something with which we must conquer coarseness,
banality, and triviality on the one hand, and stiffness, affectation,
artificiality, and unnaturalness on the other. All sorts of enemies
lurk in the development from what we are to what we must become.

Only a firm and measured connection with all that is true, all that is good, and all that is lovely and praiseworthy[68] can bring us victory in the struggle against these enemies.

This good speech, which can only be ours, has no self-existence; it is not a thing that exists apart from us. It is impossible that a coarse and uncivilized person should stand up to preach and be able to speak well. It is not so much futile as totally insufficient only to focus on one's speech when called to speak, while totally neglecting the refinement of our souls and bodies. We read that thorns bear no grapes and thistles no figs.[69] Good speech is this general refinement applied in the specific context of being called to speak in public. Be a refined person in your family, in daily life, in your social conduct, and you shall be so, with a little practice, as a speaker.

We do not make ourselves into good speakers simply by reading Cicero or Quintilian, by memorizing Schrant's rules, by weekly practice in front of a mirror. That is all good, but only if the foundation of general formation and refinement of our spirits has been laid. And how can we acquire this [eloquence], other than by interaction with the most impressive people of our generation? But then interaction in the broadest and most intimate sense: in the first place, daily engagement with the Holy Scriptures, with the prophets and apostles, with the Lord Jesus himself, who is the most beautiful of the children of men. Following this, we need engagement with the classical peoples of antiquity, whose rich culture, by the providence of God, still continues to form the basis for our development and civilization. We need engagement with the most beautiful and noble spirits from our own people and from the nations around us. Finally, but not unimportantly, we need engagement with the civilized within our own circles, and above all with the gender to whom the jewel of beauty and the secret of grace has been entrusted. Jean Paul Richter[70] has rightly said: "among girls one loses the clumsiness of the body and among women that of the mind" (unter Mädchen verliert man Ungeschicklichkeit des Körpers, unter Weibern des Geistes).

Furthermore, public speech does not simply concern a single part of our bodies; it is not restricted to voice and gestures, but rather, it takes up our whole being. The right and need of preaching is founded on the close unity of body and soul, and on the harmony of the internal and external. Bilderdijk, who had more feeling for harmony than any of our other poets, once sang beautiful verses on the necessity of agreement between the content and form of poetry.

You poet, occupied with all that spirit and art allows,
Teach dread to the happy, mix strength with weakness,
And tune your voice to the subject you paint,
That your concept be sought by the sound of your verse.

In your song let Zephyr on light wings sail,
And the stream's lapping wet softly babble its tale,
And yet the streaming wet pours out with furious thunder,
So bellows your enraged music from the pealing steam sounds.

Let the ox, under the yoke, plough the hard earth;
One feels in the tired beast, and lung and breast trudging on,
The slow and wrestling verse goes dull and slowly forth,
As also his ponderous step on every thud was heard.

The swift doe flies through the immense dales;
You follow with lightning speed and know how to catch her,
And you shoe the empty verse with swift wings!

Happily, as the language will help your effort,
And no limited choice of rhythm and syllables
Will drag you always in the prattling of forced rhymes!
Batavians, know your language and its abundance;
Master it, and you will be master of the conscience![71]

There should be one such intimate harmony between the content of the speech and its presentation. There must be harmony between body and soul, speech and voice, word and gesture, between what one says and how one says it. And what we say, we must say with all of our souls, and with all of our bodies, and all of our strength. Everything must speak to us, from us, within us. The tone of voice, the posture of the body, the movement of the hand, the eye's gaze, each has its own expression and power. Eloquence is produced by the whole person. The royal law of preaching is "give yourself, not as you are, but as you can be and must become." That is the demand of the sermon spoken by you. If that is not so, do not speak, do not tire or bother your hearers, as ultimately every kind of eloquence but the annoying kind (*le genre ennuyeux*) is good. This demands of you respect for your hearers. Nobody can demand that you give more than you are and that you have. "Whoever gives what he has is worthy of life."[72] But this can also be demanded of your words. One can never use an *odi profanum vulgus* ("I hate the common people")[73] regarding those who seek our attention. Multatuli's saying, "Public, I despise you with great fervor," should never arise in the heart of a speaker or writer and cross the barrier of his lips. The minister of the word especially must block any such superior thought from his soul, because he does not stand before a vulgar people (*vulgus*), plebeians, or a public, but rather, before the church of Christ, before the Lord's inheritance. No one, incidentally, not the aloof Horace or the proud Multatuli, really meant this declaration. The greetings at the marketplace, the applause and the waves of praise from the people were not wasted on either. Their contempt for the people is proof of their sensitivity for their acclaim.

In the sermon, which also involves the whole person, the voice takes the first place. A good voice is a precious gift. It is the echo of thought, the expression of our mind. One can laugh, as has been said for good reason, with different sounds and in so doing, give away one's nature and character. Whoever laughs with an *a*-sound and with an open mouth bears witness to his hearty character and boisterous existence. Whoever laughs with an *e*-sound has a somber frame and is unflappable. Children and naïve, fearful, indecisive adults laugh with an *i*-sound. We hear an *o*-sound in the laughter of generous and hearty people. And those who hate other people laugh with a *u*. But so is there doubtless a connection between the sound of the voice and the character of our nature. There are loud, false, rough, and gruff voices; as with a drunkard who has drowned his voice in gin (*jenever*). There are sharp, bright, and exquisite voices, which bear witness to a not all too soft disposition. There are also lovely, soft, melodious, musical voices, which capture the heart by their sound alone. It is an inestimable privilege for a speaker if he has been given a clear, powerful voice. Neander tells us regarding the holy Bernard that Germans, who could not understand his language, were nonetheless brought to tears by his voice. It is said of des Amorie van der Hoeven, just as of the old sophist Favorinus,[74] that even those who did not know a single word of Greek were delighted by his reading of Homer. The people in the church were already edified when van der Hoeven had finished reading the hymn. The voice is a fine musical instrument; blessed is the one who can play it well, and who can coax the most beautiful tones from it. But in this sense one can just as well speak falsely, as one can play and sing falsely. The highest art is that one completely and utterly controls his voice, invests the whole of his soul and every nuance of each affection in it, and through this can express himself. And that is indeed possible: the human voice is just as rich as the heart and language. It is the most beautiful and the finest music. There is no tone in the whole of nature that it cannot represent. It can rumble like thunder and blast like a hurricane. It can roar like a mountain river and burble like a creek.

But this music of the voice must be accompanied, so one might say, in the sermon by the whole of our bodies. The early preacher spoke rightly, therefore, of a "bodily eloquence" which had to illustrate, support, and confirm the thoughts of the heart in the speaker's physical posture, movement, and countenance. Not only the dramatics, but also the facial expression; not only the diction, but also action, rest on the harmony of our inner and outer person. Head and body, eye and eyebrow, hand and foot, even the clothing, must express together what is happening in our soul and is being said by our mouths.[75] No aspect of the sermon is immaterial. Each part of our body has its own language. There is a language of the lips, but also of the eyes, of the hands, of the head, and of the body. Humility and shame make the head bow, weariness makes it hang to the side, loftiness points it up, pride throws it back, shock makes it recoil. And what of our hands? Just as with our voices, with our hands we ask and answer, pray and plead, call and warn, renounce and confirm, prompt and remove, caress and detest, curse and bless. And clearer and more eloquent still than the speech of the head and hands is the language of the eye.[76] Each of the soul's affections is reflected in the eye as in a mirror. Love and hate, contempt and sympathy, friendship and anger, trust and fear, and every other passion can be read in the human eye. It glistens in joy and dulls in sorrow; it flashes in rage and shrinks in fear; it sparkles in inspiration and glazes over in despair; it becomes clearer in life and is broken in death. A single glance says more than a thousand words. Even audible speech cannot compete with the language of the eye. Whoever stands up to speak, is fixed on his paper, or keeps his gaze fixed on a single point, or like Bourdaloue[77] keeps his eyes closed, weakens the impact of his words and falls short of the demands of eloquence. The hearers rightly demand that they see the speaker, and that he sees them, and that he speaks to them not only with sound, but also with eye contact. And in so doing the perfection of the sermon is reached, when the preacher utters the same thought and speaks the same language with the content of his words, the sound of his voice, the gaze of his eye, the position of his head, the posture of his body, the gesture of his hand, even the color and cut of his clothes; when all dualism of soul and body, of internal and external, of voice and tone, of language and gesture, is caught up in perfect harmony.

All these wrong notions, which often dominate eloquence and sermon alike, are to be combated from this principle. Dramatics and facial expression have doubtless the right to exist. They are grounded in the unity of soul and body, spirit matter, internal and external, but they in no way mean to depict the matters and subjects that are named in a sermon. It would be foolish and unjust, in speaking of a zither player, to gesticulate as though plucking strings; or in speaking of a solider to assume a military posture, for example, by placing one's little finger on the seam of one's trouser leg. The preacher is not a comedian, a sermon is not a theater, and gesticulation is not a pantomime. Should this therefore be understood, Matthias Claudius[78] has no equal in giving this warning: "Distrust gesticulation and you will act 'rough and ready.'" (*Misstraue der Gestikulation und geberde dich schlecht und recht.*) Gestures are not the sermon itself; they only lead, support, and strengthen it. Every "verbose hand gesture" (*loquacitas manuum*), as Cicero so artfully names it, all hand cackle, is judged with this. Waving one's hands like a windmill brings no delight; it is idle, empty claptrap, and is thus wholly objectionable from the Christian principle.

This is my point—and with this, I return to the starting point of this lecture—that Christianity has something to tell us about eloquence and preaching. One is only eloquent if one is in accordance with the Christian principle that exists in the perfect harmony of thought and word, of word and gesture. Paul not unjustly repudiated the feigned and idle words of human wisdom. Heathendom, and also the Greeks—as Prof. Pierson[79] pointed out a few years ago—missed this deeper harmony. Dualism, contrast, and alienation always resurface in every context. In Greece there is an admirable beauty of form. The classic lines are drawn there for almost every art and science. Nature and culture go hand in hand and are interwoven so perfectly that the art itself appears to be nature.

There is an affectation of representation in epic and drama, in poetry and eloquence, in architecture and sculpture; a classic serenity of beauty is reached that fills each later generation with wonder. All these beautiful forms, however, are bearers of a short-lived content; true reality is missing. We wonder at Phidias' statue of Zeus at Olympus as a piece of art, but as a god he [Zeus] can but smile upon us. Drama reached an incomparable height, but ultimately left us ethically and aesthetically unsatisfied by the terrible might of fate playing its role therein. The German poet Lenau[80] thus rightly sang:

The art of the Greeks
Knew not the Savior and his light,
So they joked but did not mention
The pain of the deepest abyss.

That they knew not of the pain
They sought to comfort, passing gently thereover,
I recognize as the greatest magic
Bequeathed us from Antiquity.[81]

In this way, Greek philosophy sought knowledge as if with a burning thirst, but ended on the lips of Pilate with the question: "What is truth?"[82] Eloquence won various victories and became a beautiful theory with demands and rules; but all too often it took shelter in rhetoric in order to cover up the absence of inner truth. As such, the Greco-Roman peoples, like the prodigal son, finally came to feed themselves with pigs' food.

Then, though, the advent of Christianity opened up a world of thought, teeming with life and thrilling in its beauty. New content was given to art, thought received an everlasting object, and eternal content was restored to language. And now, without doubt, we may profit from the glorious form of beauty preserved for us by Greece and Rome; because everything is ours if we are Christ's— not only Paul and Cephas and Apollos, but also Homer and Horace, Demosthenes and Cicero. This reconciliation was found first in Christianity—not only the reconciliation of God and man, but also of all contrasts met in the heathen world. Everything disharmonious in thought or speech, in acting and preaching, in its essence is in conflict with Christianity. But everything in every area of art and science, whether in us or our adversaries, that is true, good, lovely, and harmonious, is Christlike. The center point of Christianity is the incarnation of the Word, and therein, the reconciliation of God and man, of spirit and matter, of content and form, of ideal and reality, of body and soul, of thought and language, of word and gesture.

THE SERMON AND THE SERVICE[1]

It always leads to melancholy when one thinks of how much our practice falls short of our Christian confession. Many good things can be pointed to, both within and outside the borders of our church: an increasing interest in the truth, which is next to godliness; a constant readiness to give toward the various tasks of Christian philanthropy; warm care for Mission and to so much more pertaining to the Christian's calling. But one should not forget to point out again and again: the tone expressed thereupon sometimes sounds high; we have not always been without boasting; and it is often the case that attention is fixed on this, with pride and self-sufficiency, and that in full view of the enemy. That should not be so. Although all of those good deeds may be gratefully recognized, that in which we fall short—and it is so much—must not fall from our sight. For those who confess Jesus the Christ, those who are members of our church in particular, a lesson must be taught: do not be high-minded, but rather, fear, be clothed with humility.

Humility, as is rightly said, is the garment that always suits us, that alone covers us, that adorns us exclusively. Whoever takes it off, in whatever circumstance, throws away his most beautiful adornment. Humility must be our home and traveling and wedding and mourning garment. In order to cultivate this Christian humility, it is good and necessary to pay attention to many things in which we fall short and that can keep us from boasting.

Think only of the sermon in the church service. The era of the powerful pulpit is no more. Churchgoing is gradually declining, not only among the moderns but also among the orthodox in most places. Interest in the church and desire to listen to a sermon is decreasing. There are now thousands who are estranged from the church, who never darken its doors, and their number increases by the day. Many who have been called orthodox have permanently given up the practice of going to church twice on a Sunday; once is more than enough for them. For many, being in church for so long, sometimes two whole hours, is even viewed as a waste of time. In our busy, calculating age, people think that this time could have been better, much better, used. We ask: How was this a waste? Could this time not better have been spent on the poor and suffering, on the children and young people? And in many places we, consciously or not, are exchanging the church service for Sunday schools and youth fellowships and home visits with the poor and miserable.

This aversion to the church should certainly be accounted for, in large part, in relation to the spirit that dominates in our time, under the influence of which one has formed a wholly wrong concept of "going to church." We live in an era of grandiose activity, an era of steam and power. It hastens and turns and pushes everything forward. We do not think about rest, silence, or calm. Whoever does not follow suit simply belongs in the past or is trampled underfoot. Time is money, and money is the soul of trade. "What do I get from it? How is it useful?" These are the questions of the day. Feverish excitement and stressed overwork are the hallmarks of all business. The silence of the holy and the calm of the eternal are all too sorely missed. "More haste, less speed" [*Festina lente*] is an old proverb. It is a rivalry, a competition to be the fastest. This spirit has also left its mark on Christians. Despite their confession of an ancient faith, they are also children of the era. An industrious, active Christianity is now appearing. Sitting in silence under the word, which should have been their strength, has fallen from their thoughts. If you are a Christian, [you must] show your faith in your works, say what you do, what you give, what you achieve. And it is certainly the case that whoever fails to praise all this Christian endeavor unconditionally is deemed by many to be loveless or lacking in faith.

As a consequence of this, all that pertains to the still life of faith is moved to the background and fades away. We can no longer devote ourselves to attentive examination of the "footsteps" of the spiritual life, to the fine and precise distinction between the true and false faith and life, to the wide summary of the marks and characteristics of the true Christian. Now there is something else to do. Christianity must make its power known not in depth, but rather in length and breadth. And as such, we no longer have the time or desire to go to church twice on the day of rest, sometimes to spend an hour listening to a sermon from the mouth of a teacher whom we have heard so often. What could be exciting or useful there? There, we are, it is said, much too passive and can do too little; [in this context] we are almost deemed too young for and incapable of anything; in the church service our portion is too slight. We will still certainly listen to a lecture, a popular address, or a speech on education or missions by a celebrated speaker from whom one can learn something new and can hear something outstanding. But our impatient and cultured generation can no longer take listening to a sermon that always handles the same subject and that lacks all the attractiveness of novelty. Athenian curiosity and a high sense of spiritual development are also qualities found among many orthodox churchgoers.

Why one goes to church and what one has to do there, you see, have been almost entirely forgotten. The right concept of the public church service is being lost. The idea that we have something substantial to do in the church service, that we are not passive, that we are busy and active, that we go there to carry out priestly work, to be occupied with our Father's business, to sacrifice in the temple of the Lord, to offer to God ourselves and all that is ours, not only to establish ourselves and to become established, but so that we and others might be truly established and built up in the most holy faith, is misunderstood. That is the true meaning of going up to the house of prayer. All believers are priests—therein lies the key to this declaration. And now the work of priests no longer consists—as Van Andel[2] recently so truthfully and beautifully wrote in No. 19 of *Maranatha*—in the mediating work of the Old Covenant, such belongs to that special priesthood, but falls away as the priesthood is widened. But this still remains: the observation of service in the sanctuary—namely, the sacrifice, or more precisely still, the heavenly spiritual sacrifice, the sacrifice made from the perspective of the New Covenant. This sacrifice consists of the confession of Christ's name, in the worship of God, in the community of Christ's intercession, and in offering up gifts in service of God's work and of Christ's poor brothers. It is now God's will that he be called on openly and collectively: openly, because such is in agreement with his worth, and because it is fitting that the world hears when God is recognized as the God of his people; and collectively, because God only desires and recognizes believers as the body of Christ, organized wholly in Christ, and does not want fellowship with the individual outside of that body, which is outside of Christ, as in the former time with an Israelite who separated himself from Israel. Thus, the [church's] gathering takes place on the day of rest. Each local congregation represents the body of Christ. Its members are called to priestly service in the congregation, which is in the holy place of God. They gather as priests, bring sacrifices of praise and thanksgiving, and petitions and requests, to God; they bring their gifts for the church and their brothers. That is the essence, the glorious direction, the pleasure of our gatherings on Sunday, or whenever they occur. As such, we are placed in community with the heavenly congregation and are joined with it in *one* work, for which reason the angels, as a sign of this unity, are present both in our gatherings and in the heavenly gathering.

The question is, however: Where is this so understood and practiced? Certainly not where one only goes to church to hear a preacher; where one does not think that there is anything else to be done in church (namely, priestly service) and imagines that he is passive and needs to do nothing but be built up; where one stays at home if the preacher stays at home (as though nothing remains in the sanctuary if the preacher is not preaching); where the collection offering costs us nothing, and where the gift is no greater than we would give a beggar at our door; and where in place of seeing hymns as worship, one does not sing along, or rather, one bellows along heartlessly and thoughtlessly.

These are words that may not be forgotten, that must be guarded in the heart. The preacher's calling, especially in the present day—now that this true attitude [toward worship] is being lost—is to teach people the meaning of the church service. They must draw the attention of their hearers, the members of the congregation, away from themselves, and be aware that one should not go to church simply to hear preachers, that preaching is not the highest and only feature [of the church service], and that rather, we gather together as believers, in order to serve together as priests and to offer God praise and adoration, love, and gifts. If that would be better understood, churchgoing would be more highly esteemed, and the younger generation would not become estranged from the church.

However much guilt for this increasing fault lies with the congregation, which (under the influence of the spirit of the age) fails to recognize its glorious calling, a significant part of the guilt belongs to the preachers themselves. The sermon is certainly not the only, or even the most important part of our worship service—that is the priestly work of the believers together—but it is nonetheless the high point of the priestly gathering and worship. An enormous amount depends on the preaching: in our exercise of religion, it is the greatest and highest part. While one could call the Roman Church the Church of the Mass, the Protestant churches are the churches of the word. The thought that Jesus wishes to rule only through his word and Spirit is glorious and beautiful. He despises swords and clubs, chains and prisons, violence and trickery; he only wants to win this rule by the moral, spiritual weapons of word and Spirit. And particularly so through the means of the *preached* word: not the word read or sung, but rather the spoken word. Faith is by *hearing*.[3] Therefore, it is not at all fastidiousness or obstinacy if the people want their preacher to speak to them, and not simply to read a sermon before them.

The Lord has joined his blessing to the preaching of his word. It is by this preaching that the congregation remains strong and has done so throughout history. Through preaching, in connection to the signs and seals of the covenant, the congregation is strengthened and built up in the most holy faith and incorporated in the body of Christ. Through preaching, the congregation is protected in its purity, encouraged in its battle, healed in its sufferings, established in its confession. Through preaching, the flock remains with the church, and the church with the flock in increasing authority and respect and worship.

The meaning of preaching cannot easily be overestimated, nor can the worth of the office of preacher. To be a *verbi divini minister*, servant of the Divine Word, one who shares from the hiddenness of God, who declares words of eternal life—which earthly position could be compared to this? The responsibility and the calling are thus also greater for the bearer. In these days there are also reasonable complaints regarding the devaluing felt regarding both church and churchgoing, a prominent part of which is the responsibility of the servants of the word.

Whoever makes himself something of a connoisseur of the fruits and products of preaching finds abundant material for complaint. Certainly, one must be reasonable. We cannot judge preachers and sermons by the same standard as orators and lecturers. It must be remembered that there are many congregations, and thus many preachers. Demanding that they should all be orators is simply to find fault with the will of God, who only gives the glorious gift of eloquence to a few. We must also remember that the minister of the word must speak twice on Sundays, and still on other occasions during the week. Thus when he is performing his other duties earnestly, he cannot always be fresh and recent and new.

But having taken all of this into consideration, how much still remains regarding the form and content of preaching about which one can complain! The reason for this is not that someone does not have greater gifts, but that he does not put [the gifts he has] to better use. This happens so often. How many fail to make the most of their gifts, but squander and misuse them! Often there are cliché and affectation in term and tone, false accents and coarse expressions, unnatural posturing and gesticulation. By way of content there is often a lack of earnest preparation, simplicity and truth, pace and thought, faith and inspiration, and above all, solemnity and unction.

All this taken together, we can safely say that preaching is, at present, out of touch with the time and does not meet its needs. If the pulpit is to become a mighty force once again, this situation must be remedied, and that will happen when we return to searching the Holy Scriptures.

That is the primary lack of contemporary preaching; it is not drawn out of the Scriptures; it is not baptized in their spirit. At present there is research in Scripture: in the academies, the introductory sciences play the largest role in this. But that is not real research. Through it, one learns a great deal about the Scriptures: one perhaps becomes familiar with the *milieu* in which they came into existence, the foundation from which they arose. But while this study brings us that advantage, and although it does not lead us, as do so many things, to doubt and suspicion, it does not teach us Scripture itself in its richness and depth, in its unity and diversity. And then our preaching becomes idle. Then our preaching loses the power and authority that it needs and that it can borrow only from the word of God, upon which it is stands. In that case, our preaching may be a work of art, an adornment with neat divisions, a molded thing in a neat form—but it will nonetheless be poor, as it lacks the eternal content of God's word. Study of the Scriptures is thus the first and primary demand upon the preacher: organized, persistent, continual study of the Holy Scriptures, if need be without commentaries, but with a clear view, with a praying heart, with a pious, receptive soul, with a sanctified and purified conscience.

Oh, we still know so little of Holy Scripture. We understand but a little portion of it. It contains as yet hidden treasures that have never been enjoyed by the congregation. We have had a grab at it here and there, and eighteen centuries have already passed, and time winds on toward its end! We must hasten ourselves, so that when the Son of Man comes, we will understand the signs of the times and declare them in the light of prophecy; so that we can say to him that we have held his word and have not denounced his name; and that we will know him and the power of his resurrection and the fellowship of his sufferings.[4] Each of us, especially preachers, has something of our own to contribute to this: to make God's word known, to make our preaching more and more subservient to this.

The congregation must understand Scripture better, encounter it more clearly, and understand it more in its organic and coherent interconnectivity. That will bring the advantage that the congregation will be more firmly established against the doubts and theories regarding unbelief in our era, and the younger generation will not become estranged from the truth that is next to godliness.

If ministers of the word practice this demand, all the other shortcomings that currently disfigure preaching will gradually decline. And then everything else will follow. That wretched "motto-preaching,"[5] which is so often used to declare mere opinions to the people under the guise of God's word, will cease. And then, regardless of all of our own thoughts and fancies, nothing but the healthy, fresh, strengthening food of the word of God will be extended to the people. The preacher will need entertain no fear of burnout, and neither shall he spend hours and days looking for a text and material; nor will the listeners complain about lack of freshness and paucity and boredom. The people have the right to be fed and refreshed spiritually each Sunday. Give them something to eat, chimes the lesson for preachers, but do not simply fill their stomachs with the shifting opinions and novelties of the day. Rather, give them the firm nourishment and strengthening food of God's word. Then the content will gradually become healthy and living and fresh, when it is drawn from the Bible. The form [of the sermon] will also benefit. It can be no other way. Whoever earnestly studies Holy Scripture must set aside all arrogance, haughtiness, and idle philosophy. The Bible is the most simple, natural, comprehensible book in the world; completely popular, a book of the people like no other. Study of the Bible will make us popular in the best, most noble sense of the word: popular in the sense that we refrain from all coarseness, roughness, and indelicacy, but also that we strike the tone that touches the heart of the people and makes the snares of their souls tremble. Then our speech will be formed by, and indeed will become *one* with the speech of the Holy Scriptures, which is the speech of the best Preacher, the only Teacher, the *Doctor et Consolator Ecclesiae* [Doctor and Counsellor of the Church], the Holy Spirit. Then we will speak to the people, not to be wondered at by them, but to be understood by them. Then we will speak not for our own sake, but for theirs. Then our preaching will no longer be boring, monotone, and irritating. Rather, we will speak full of the Holy Spirit, in a demonstration of power;[6] then we will speak no words of human wisdom, but rather the eternal, lasting word of our God. The fruit of such preaching is inevitable. His word never returns empty.[7]

In addition to this, the congregation deserves as much, that we open and declare God's word to it. It has the right to this. It is made up of people who must work each day, and who have almost no time left over to study the Holy Scriptures. On Sundays they long for their ministers to open the Scriptures and unravel the secrets found therein. They long for this to be clear, intelligible, and comprehensible, not in miserable reasoning, but in simplicity and power, in their own language and prepared with their understanding in mind. And they compensate and soothe [the cost of] this effort and diligence more than twofold; not perhaps in silver and gold, but in more than these: in their estimations and love and gratitude, which cost more than all the treasures of the earth.

And also with regard to material things, it will go well with us. A good sermon never goes without its reward. If the congregation sees that we give ourselves to them, they will give themselves to us. If we work for their spiritual salvation, they will not let our physical lives fall into need. The congregation will not be ungrateful as long as we, as their preachers, preach in search of God's honor and the salvation of their souls. The preaching of God's word, pure, unadulterated, in simplicity and truth, in faith and with enthusiasm, is also the preservation and guarantee of the existence and growth of *De Vrije Kerk*.[8]

THE WORLD-CONQUERING POWER OF FAITH

A Sermon on 1 John 5:4b preached in the Burgwalkerk in Kampen on June 30, 1901.[1]

This sermon was preached on the occasion of President Kruger,[2] with his retinue, being present in the gathering of the congregation during his visit to Kampen, on Sunday 30th June 1901. Many who heard it made known their desire that it should appear in published form. Although I could not literally give the sermon again, I have no objections to complying with this friendly request. The whole is now given concisely, in agreement with the words spoken on that day.

—Herman Bavinck

The nineteenth century, which lies only a few months behind us, has been rightly named by many as the century of unbelief and revolution.[3] But although we have barely entered the twentieth century, we feel the question rise up within us involuntarily: might this new century allow us to see a return to the Christian faith and an application of the principles of the Reformation to every area of life?

There are three signs above all that make this question arise in our hearts. In the first place, with the turn of the century there is also a noticeable shift in the current of thinking and striving among the nations. The revolution has failed to meet expectation; almost none of its promises have been fulfilled, the paradise that it dangled before our eyes has yet to be built on this earth. Rather, disappointment and dissatisfaction prevail everywhere. People are tired of life; on the one hand there is a lack of satisfaction with culture, and on the other, a sense of discontent and bitter complaint against the state of society. And while many, such as the radicals and the socialists, expect salvation only from a stricter and broader application of the principles of the revolution, there are also those who (in increasing numbers) recoil from the practical consequences of the doctrine of unbelief, and who once again incline to the inclusion of a place for religion in the various spheres of human life. Interest in religion among many of the children of our age has evidently returned. In the place of audacious denial, there is a recognition of and regard for the unseen. We can even see a striving to follow long inaccessible paths from the appearance of things to their essence, to go from the visible world to its mysterious background, to that which sustains it. The problems with this new intellectual trend being noted, it nonetheless contains something that gives cause for happiness and thankfulness. The rule of the intellect has come to an end; the conscience [*gemoed*] has retaken its rights; faith has won its first victory over the worship of the material and the tyranny of reason.

The second occurrence, which deserves our attention and gives reason to the question above, is the war in South Africa.[4] Many wars have been waged during and at the close of the previous century, but among them there is none that has so deeply and widely awoken interest as that of the two South African Republics in order to retain their freedom and independence. In the first place, we should certainly look for reason in the clear fact that in no other war in recent times have justice and power been so sharply outlined against each other, as in this fight by a small people against a powerful state. It is because England aggrieved [a broad] sense of justice in the vilest manner that all peoples, with their sympathy, practical support, and prayers, sided almost unanimously with the oppressed Afrikaners. But this interest, which was inspired by this aggrieved sense of justice, was also accompanied by admiration for the simple, powerful faith witnessed to at the heart of the heroic Boer fighters in this struggle. While unbelief was growing rapidly in the civilized world, a people in South Africa suddenly stood up, few in number, small in power, unpracticed in organized warfare, but strong through its faith, inspired by zeal for justice, prepared for any sacrifice for freedom, however costly. And that faith stunned the world and showed its strength over violence and might.

The third event, finally, that speaks to us about the power of faith is the result of political elections in our own land.[5] It is beyond doubt that strange fire has been brought to the altar in this service, which we, as citizens, were to have directed for God's glory. Far from all who took part in this work let their choice be defined by the demand of Christian principles. But nonetheless, we may rejoice at the outcome of the elections and, whether also with trembling, be glad. Whoever compares the beginning of this century with the previous, sees the bravest expectations surpassed. God has done well by his people in this land, caused [his people] to expand and be established from day to day, over and above all praise and thanksgiving. And now, according to the result of the elections, the people of the Netherlands have declared by great majority: we do not want to follow the path of unbelief and revolution any further; and also for the government of our land we desire that Christian principles be taken into account. Our people have pushed a beautiful confession through the ballot box. And in that confession a victory over the world has been won by faith.

These three occurrences have led me to the resolution to speak to you, in this hour, on the world-conquering power of faith, while the president of the South African Republic and his following are gathered in this place with the church of Christ in the house of prayer. Let us, however, present ourselves in thanksgiving and prayer before the Lord's countenance and invoke a blessing from him over our gathering!

> *And this is the victory that has overcome the world—our faith.*
> (1 John 5:4b)

John is normally, and not without reason, named the apostle of love. But this does not in the least exclude [the fact that] he constantly deals with faith. In the first five verses of our chapter, he bears witness to three glorious things about faith. First he says that faith implants a new principle of living in the person. Whoever believes that Jesus is the Christ has been born of God. Through faith he has gone over from death to life; he does not belong any more to below, but rather to above; he belongs no more to the world but is rather a child of God, a citizen of heaven, an heir of eternal life. Because, as many as have received Jesus as the Christ, he has given the right to be called children of God—namely, those who believe in his name, those born not by blood or the will of the flesh or the will of man, but of God.

Second, John witnesses that faith in Jesus as the Christ is a mighty power toward love and obedience to God's commandments. Whoever believes that Jesus is the Christ, the Son of God, has therein experienced the great love that God, in the sending of his Son and making reconciliation through his blood, has revealed to us. And the experience of this matchless love compels him to love the One who gave him birth, with all his soul and mind and powers. Because God is the First: herein is love, not that we had loved God, but that he loved us and sent his Son to be the propitiation for our sins. Thus, after this we also love him, because he first loved us. And whoever loves God with thankful love in return also loves all those who with him have been born of God and belong to the same Father's family. Yes, by faith he receives a deep desire to walk in all, and not merely some, of God's commandments uprightly. And these commandments are not heavy. The world's commandments are heavy; serving the world is hard. But for whoever loves God, his commandments are a pleasure throughout the day. For his disciples, Jesus' yoke is easy and his burden is light.

And third, John assures us then in the fourth and fifth verses of our chapter that faith is a power that even overcomes the world. Everyone who is born of God overcomes the world. He overcomes the world through faith—namely, through faith that Jesus is God's Son. We will see this *world-conquering faith*, we hope, when we pay attention to, consecutively,

The *opposition* that this faith experiences.
The *character* that this faith bears.
The *victory* that is promised to this faith.

I.

Everything that stands against faith, all the opposition that it experiences, the whole might of enmity against which it strives, is summed up together by John under the name "the world." The Greek word translated as "world" actually means "jewel" [or "adornment"] and points out that the people who spoke this language saw the world in its beautiful aspect. Because of the richness of its forms and colors, its harmonious order and regularity, the Greeks marveled at it as a work of art, as a work of beauty.

The Holy Scriptures are also aware of this beauty found in the world. They narrate to us what the Greek philosophers did not suppose regarding the furthest horizon: that the almighty and eternal God, who called things that were not, to be as though they were, created the whole world by his word, and that he, having come to the end of his creative work, saw all that he had made, and saw that it was very good. But also, after the fall, the Scriptures often sing of the beauty of the world in mighty, devotional language. The heavens declare God's glory and the firmament his handiwork. The voice of God is on the mighty waters. His breath renews the face the earth. His footsteps overflow with abundance.[6] Even the human, made a little lower than the angels, is crowned with honor and glory.[7] The Lord is good to all, his name is glorious over all the earth, his mercies are over all his works.

But nonetheless, the Scriptures do not stop at this aesthetic worldview. They differ indeed massively from the heathen deification of nature, as they [the Scriptures] marvel at God's work in the vast creation and make famous his virtues. But it is not enough for [the Scriptures] to praise the beauty of the world. They set a different, higher, moral bar against the created, and test everything by the demands of Divine righteousness. And then, building on this standard, they pronounce that this world is not what it should be. It is fallen and has been stripped of its ideal. The creation has become a world that stands against God and has put itself in service of sin. The fallen angels belong to the world in this sense, those who, situated beautifully at the foot of God's throne, nonetheless did not keep their principle. To this world belong people who have all fallen in their [covenantal] head, and are therefore conceived and born in sin, and daily increase their guilt before God. To this world belongs the human understanding, which is darkened; the will, which is inclined to evil; the heart, from which all evil thoughts come forth; the soul, which has turned away from God and clings to the material; the body, which uses all of its members as weapons for unrighteousness. To it belongs everything set up by men and brought into being by men: the institutions of family and society and state, the works of calling and business, of science and art, of industry and commerce. To it belongs the whole of humanity, from the first man to the last, all born from a single woman; in all its generations and families and languages and peoples; in all of these eras of its history, through all the centuries of its development and expansion; in its struggles and triumphs, in its civilizing and decay, in the states that it founds, in the empires that it establishes. To it belongs even the senseless and lifeless creation—because the earth has been cursed due to the human will, the whole creation sighs and is in labor pains until now. [The creation] is subject to vanity, not willingly, but on the will of the one who has subjected it to vanity.

The existing order of created beings, in its entirety, the whole orrery[8] that is God's creation, that fixed whole in all its visible and invisible parts, insofar as it is an instrument of unrighteousness, is summed up by the apostle John under the name "the world." And he can name it as such, in *one* name, with *one* word, because sin has damaged the whole world and makes it (in its entirety) live from *one* principle, inspired by *one* spirit, pointed toward *one* goal: namely, enmity and rebellion against God, its Creator and Lord.

Oh, we say from day to day, and pronounce without thought, that God is love. And he is just that, eternal love and matchless comfort. For God so loved even this guilty and lost world that he gave his only begotten Son, so that whoever believes in him should not perish but have everlasting life. Still, outside of Christ, who dares to boast of God's love? Does not the whole of nature preach to us, and does not our own heart and mind preach to us, that God's favor does not rest on his creatures, that he has a dispute with his creation, that all creatures pass away through his wrath and are terrified by his anger?

Is that not an alarming situation? God and the world at odds with each other because of sin! A state of enmity and hatred, of dispute and war between the Creator and his creatures, between the Maker and the made, between the almighty, eternal God and the powerless creature that is nothing but dust and ashes and has no existence in and of itself. This world, in its entirety, rests not on its own foundation, but is rather maintained from moment to moment by the word of God's power. He gives it all its being and life, all its capacity and strength, all that it is and all that it has. Satan would also have no might were it not given him from above. And yet sin organizes the whole universe with all the creatures and powers therein as an instrument against God and his kingdom. From all this sin makes a world that has the prince of darkness as its commander, that lies in evil, that lives in a state of injustice, that forms a kingdom of sin and unrighteousness, and that seeks to triumph over God by violence and trickery, over his name and his kingdom.

And precisely through this, sin taking all of God's creations and gifts into its service, the world forms such an almost limitless power. Who is equipped to stand against its domination, to break free from its influence? Could a creature, walled in on every side by the world and bound in its snares, do that? Could a person, who belongs to this world with all his body and soul, with all his thought and desire, do that? After all, this world is not only external to us; it lives within us in the highest place, in our hearts, in our understanding, in our will, and in all our affections. And therefore it has power over us, seducing us by the desires of the flesh and the desires of the eye and the pride of life,[9] none of which come from the Father, but rather are of the world. Everyone who sins is a slave to sin.[10]

No, we do not serve the world willy-nilly. At the core of our being we do not stand against it on God's side, although we sometimes gladly delude ourselves [in that regard]. We are all by nature children of wrath, without God and without Christ, without hope in the world. We are, as people, the most prominent part of that fallen world. In us it has its strongest proof, its mightiest warriors. We serve it voluntarily and willingly with all the abilities God gives us, with all the powers he loans us. We follow its direction without opposition. We stand guilty, impure, tainted, condemned before God's countenance, with the whole world. It is in us and around us as an undeniable power; it extends the scepter of its dominion over all creation. Miserable people that we are, who shall then save us from the might of this world? Who will free us from the guilt of sin, from the stain of impurity, from subservience to wickedness, from the violence of the grave? Who can restore to us mastery over the world and crown us as winners over it?

II.

See, beloved, as we people stand desperately and vainly look to creatures for salvation, John, the apostle of the Lord Jesus Christ, comes to us and holds God's word before our eyes: this is the victory that has overcome the world—namely, our faith.

Faith, the victory over the world!

When we first hear this, we could feel the thought arising within us that John is mocking our misery, has no idea of the world's might, and has an insufficiently scientific view of faith. Faith, so it is said anyway, may be something more than an opinion, but it is still far less than knowledge and never leads to more than a certain degree of probability. And such faith, which is nothing more than an uncertain, unsteady opinion, should be the victory over the world, not over a single thought or desire, but over the whole world and all its power, with which it masters us from within and without.

Is it not more sensible to act like Naaman the Syrian, who, when commanded by Elisha to wash himself seven times in the Jordan in order to be healed, became furious, saying: "Are not Abana and Pharpar, the rivers of Damascus, better than all the rivers in Israel? Can I not wash myself in them and be clean?"[11] We run this risk when we learn that John gives us no weapon in this fight but faith, and we walk away saying: "Are states and kingdoms, the arts and sciences, the discoveries and inventions brought about by men, not better weapons than the simple faith that John commends to us in this war?" Why, if he wants to equip us for this battle against the world, does he not name science, which man masters over all the works of God's hands? Why does he not name art, a mighty skill and the highest and most beautiful thought of men embodied in the stubborn material world? Why does he not name states, which bridle the human's inner wild animal and coerce him to walk in the path of righteousness? Why does he not name empires, which bind their peoples to the victory train of tyrants and tie all lands together in one area? Why does he name nothing about the glory and greatness of men and speak only of faith shared by a few?

Still, before anger leads us to give up on John's word, let us carefully weigh up what he means by this faith and why he attributes such a world-conquering power to it. Earnest, impartial research forbids us from being deceived by the appearance of things. If we only imagine the fight found here, the issue at hand changes in character. This is a world of sin and unrighteousness, of destruction and death, and it must be overcome. And whatever laurels science may have gained in its sphere, it has never freed a single soul from guilt and made it appear without fear before God's face. However art has made things more pleasant in human life, it has never provided a single creature with the only comfort by which you may live and die. And whatever conquests states and empires have won over men and peoples, they have never changed the heart and in free obedience submitted themselves to the will of the King of kings. All of these weapons, used by men, have been borrowed from this world, are taken out of this world, and also pass away with this world. Conceived and born in sin, they are all often in service of the world and have furthered its power and extended its dominance.

But the faith that John speaks of tells of other victories. It has an entire history behind it, a history that begins with a lost paradise and that continues from generation to generation. Let just a few of the heroes of the faith pass by your spirit for but a moment! By faith Noah, being warned by God concerning events as yet unseen, in reverent fear constructed an ark for the saving of his household. By this he condemned the world and became an heir of the righteousness that comes by faith.[12] By faith Abraham obeyed when he was called to go out to a place that he was to receive as an inheritance. And he went out, not knowing where he was going.[13] By faith Moses, when he was grown up, refused to be called the son of Pharaoh's daughter, choosing rather to be mistreated with the people of God than to enjoy the fleeting pleasures of sin. He considered the reproach of Christ greater wealth than the treasures of Egypt, for he was looking to the reward.[14] By faith the people crossed the Red Sea as on dry land, but the Egyptians, when they attempted to do the same, were drowned. By faith the walls of Jericho fell down after they had been encircled for seven days.[15] By faith Paul entered the heathen world and planted the banner of the gospel of the cross at the center point of civilization. By faith the church of Christ withstood the Roman Empire in the first centuries, and led the peoples of Europe to obey Christ. By faith Luther lifted up his voice against the degeneration of Rome's church and set the pure light of the gospel to shine anew. By faith, our forefathers fought for eighty years against Roman idolatry and Spanish tyranny, and won the victory of freedom against both. By faith, the heroes of South Africa bound the weapons of all-powerful England for freedom and justice, and to the amazement of the watching world have remained standing to the present day. By faith—whom else should I name from all of those thousands, the thousands upon thousands, who in the passage of time have conquered kingdoms, enforced justice, obtained promises, stopped the mouths of lions, quenched the power of fire, escaped the edge of the sword, were made strong out of weakness, became mighty in war, put foreign armies to flight?[16]

Recognize history, then, as a witness to the world-conquering power of faith! But such a witness does not set aside the [particular] history of each [kind of] faith, [it does not deal] with faith simply as a psychological phenomenon, regardless of its object, origin, and essence. Because there are many sorts of faith. There is a faith that comes from within a person, that belongs to the world, that bows before idols, that is simply a form of unbelief or superstition, that does not fight against and conquer the world, but rather that supports and establishes it. John, the apostle of the Lord, ascribes world-conquering power only to the faith shared with his brothers and sisters, to the belief that Jesus is the Christ, the Son of the living God. Only this certain, defined faith is equipped for victory, because that faith maintains that *Jesus* the Son of God is the Christ. Jesus, which is to say, that historic person, that person born of a woman, who nineteen centuries ago lived in Palestine, who was like us in every way, but without sin, who went throughout the land preaching and doing good works and healing every sickness among the people, who lay down his life on the scornful and scandalous cross. It maintains that this Jesus, who, when he came into our midst, would not have been seen by anyone as more than a man, that this Jesus, not being beautiful in form or having any glory that we should desire him,[17] that he, notwithstanding all this, is God's Son, the Only Begotten of the Father, full of grace and truth, of the patriarchs according to the flesh, but also truly God over all, blessed forever.[18] It maintains that this Jesus is the Christ, and not our virtues or good works, not the art of science, not the state or power, not a single creature on heaven or on earth, but rather that he alone is the Christ, the Servant of the Lord, the Anointed One of God, the one who makes atonement for sins, the Savior of the world, our highest Prophet, our only High Priest, our eternal King.

And through this, through its content and object, is faith precisely a world-conquering power. It is no mere work of the lips or a rational assent to a historical truth. But it is firm certainty, unshakeable conviction, ineradicable confidence, not of blood or of the will of the flesh, not of the will of a man, but coming from God and worked in the heart by his Spirit. It is the bond that the soul binds to the Mediator and holds fast to him as seeing the Unseen. It is the power that transfers the person from darkness to the Kingdom of the Son of God's love and gives him a point of support and rest in the world of immovable realities. It is the firm ground for the things that he hopes and the irrefutable proof for the things that he does not see.[19] It is the courage by which he faces up to the whole world and rejoices: If God is *for* us, who can be against us?[20] It is the comfort that makes him sing psalms by night and also causes the song to rise up during the most frightful oppression:

> The Lord is my strength and my song;
>   he has become my salvation.
> Glad songs of salvation
>   are in the tents of the righteous:
> "The right hand of the Lord does valiantly,
> the right hand of the Lord exalts,
> the right hand of the Lord does valiantly!"[21]

III.

Because it is in *that* faith—namely, faith in Jesus as the Christ—that victory over the world is thus promised and assured.

In its principle and essence, it is already victory over the world. It defeats the world not only in its consequences and fruit, but is from its first beginning onward already victory over the world. Believing that Jesus is the Christ is the simplest thing that can be thought, the only fresh and living way for a guilty child of man to participate in heavenly blessedness, eternal life, and peace with God by mere grace.

But this does not deny that there is so much needed to receive and practice that faith that no man can give himself or acquire it.

To believe in truth that Jesus is the Christ requires that we deny ourselves, that we crucify our flesh with its desires, capture our understanding with all its thoughts and lead it to obedience, consider all our righteousness as throwaway rags, accuse ourselves of trespassing all the commandments, give up on our hope in each created thing, fully recognize God's justice, and plead on his grace alone! How much arises to oppose such believing! Everything sets itself against this, everything in us and outside of us. Our understanding and our heart, our will and affections, our flesh and blood, our name and our standing, our money and our goods, our location and society, the whole world in us and outside of us, and then above all Satan, who is the master of this world, the god of this century, who dazzles the senses. In order to believe, we must be crucified to the world and the world must be crucified to us.

But therefore [faith] is victory over the world, also in its origin and essence. Whoever believes has received a new life. He has become a new creation; he is called from darkness to God's wonderful light; he is no longer a citizen, a subject of the world, but rather he is born of God, of his Spirit, from above. His citizenship is in heaven. His unrighteousness is forgiven; his infirmity is healed; his life is saved from damnation; he is crowned with goodness and mercy. Who shall bring accusations against the elect of God? God is the one who makes righteous.[22] Who is to condemn? Christ Jesus is the one who died—more than that, who was raised—who is at the right hand of God, who indeed is interceding for us. Who shall separate us from the love of Christ? Shall tribulation, or distress, or persecution, or famine, or nakedness, or danger, or sword? But in all these things we are more than conquerors through him who loved us.[23]

By faith the believer first separates himself from the violence of the world, but in addition to this he has mastery over that world with a prophetic and priestly and kingly power. The belief that Jesus is the Christ is, after all, no rigid rest; it does not withdraw into the stillness of isolation, but rather it is living and power and breaks into the world, full of valor. It does not only enjoy; it works: it says something and it does something. It witnesses and it saves. It speaks and it acts. It attacks with the power of the word; it stands up in a demonstration of the spirit and of power.[24] Who believes cannot remain silent. In the midst of the world they let the witness go out that Jesus is the Christ. They declare no wisdom of their own, but preach wisdom that is from above, even though that may appear as foolishness in the eyes of the world. They bear witness that Jesus is the Christ, nothing else, nothing less, nothing more. Jesus the Christ, and not gold or power, not violence and coercion, not fame and virtue, not science and art, but Jesus alone is the Savior of the world, the only, the perfect, the wholly sufficient Savior, and no one or nothing next to him or beneath him or alongside him.

And through that witness is faith once again a world-conquering power, because the world has nothing to which it can bear witness. It does not believe and therefore cannot bear witness. It does not know the power of the word. As soon as the church carries its confession into the world, [the world] grasps for the weapons of degradation and coercion, of abuse and oppression. These are the weapons the world has in its war against the church of Christ. But faith is strong by its witness alone. It does not call names, it does not rage, and it does not pursue. It only bears witness, fast, certain, unshakeable, unremitting, until its last hour, until sent to the burning stake. It is like a rock standing in the midst of the waves. Let the world come at it with all the clatter of its weapons and show of force! No violence or coercion, no frame for a funeral pyre, can stand against rock-solid faith. It glories in oppression. It triumphs in its defeat. It rises again from death. The blood of the martyrs is the seed of the church.[25]

But faith does not only bear witness; it also works and acts. It works through love. Love is the fruit: the ripe, glorious, precious fruit of faith. Whoever believes that Jesus is the Christ has experienced God's love and therefore loves the One who gave him birth; because whoever does not have love has not known God, because God is love.[26] Whoever believes has only love for those who with him have been born of God and believe in Jesus' name, because we know that we have gone over from death to life because we love our brothers. Whoever does not love his brother remains in death. Whoever believes loves God's commandments, because this is love for God: that we obey his commandments; and his commandments are not heavy, they are all fulfilled by love.

And through this love faith is also a power that conquers the world; because the world does not know the secret of love, it hates both Jesus and his Father, and it hates all those to whom Christ has given his Father's word, because they are not of this world. But the church of Christ is mighty when it loves its enemies by the command and requirement of its Master; blessing those who curse it, doing good to those who hate it, and praying for those who violently persecute it. Love is stronger than death, it drives away all of these fears, it covers over and believes and hopes and bears all things, and it never passes away.

All of this world-conquering faith, however, derives faith not from itself but from Christ alone. Therefore, it is finally the perfect victory over the world, because it is faith in Christ, the Father's Anointed One. Everything points to him. Everything depends on him; he is the content and the object, he is also the giver and sustainer, the author and perfecter of the faith. In faith, we confess simply that he and he alone conquers the world. He has conquered. Even *before* his death, he called to his disciples: "In the world you will have tribulation. But take heart; I have overcome the world."[27] He has overcome it through the suffering of his death; in dying he triumphed over it; he triumphed over governments and powers through the cross. And he goes forth triumphant, in order that he might triumph. Now he fights from heaven at his Father's right hand against the world through the faith of his church, which is his army, and which is prepared by him from above with gifts and powers, with the belt of truth, with the breastplate of righteousness, with the shield of faith, with the helmet of salvation, with the sword of the Spirit.[28] And he shall be victorious at the end of days, because he must rule as King, until all his enemies are set under his feet. Then, at the end of the ages when he shall find almost no faith on the earth, he himself shall come to strike the final blow and subdue all his enemies. In that hour every knee shall bow before him and every tongue confess that he is Lord, to the glory of God the Father.

*

Brothers and sisters, do you have that faith? Do you know that faith in its wondrous, world-conquering power? You bear the name of believers, but are you indeed what you are called? Paul encourages the church in Corinth: "Examine yourselves to see whether you are in the faith; test yourselves! Or do you not realize that Christ is in you?—unless indeed you fail to meet the test."[29] And a failure, worthy to be disowned, is everyone who lives at peace with the world and has not yet joined the fight against it. The love of the Father is not in those who love the world. Whoever is a friend of the world is called an enemy of God.[30]

The fight against the world is indeed frightening and hard. It is a fight against flesh and blood, against thoughts and temptations. But it is a good and noble fight. Many wars are waged on this earth, between peoples and nations. And some of them, though far from all, not even the majority, but still some, in spite of all their miseries and regrets, are to be seen as noble and great. Noble and great is the fight on behalf of women and children, for home and hearth, for king and country, for freedom and for justice. Our fathers' fight was noble and great. The fights of both South African Republics were noble and great; may God bless their weapons and quickly lead them to a complete triumph! But however noble and great some wars might have been, they were nonetheless waged only for one justice or another, a holy justice quite certainly, but still for a limited part of justice and freedom.

But here is a fight for nothing less than justice, for God's justice, for righteousness itself in its principle and essence, for perfect freedom, for the highest and holiest good that could ever befall a person. It is the noblest, the most beautiful, the most glorious battle in which a human can fight. It is a fight against the world and against everything that is of the world, against ourselves, against our money and our possessions, against all the lust of the flesh and lust of the eyes and the pride of life.[31]

But it is also a fight for our own salvation, for the salvation of our souls, for a heavenly inheritance, for the crown of righteousness, which the Righteous Judge will give to all who have fought the good fight and completed the race. It is a fight for justice, for the truth, for freedom, for Christ and his kingdom, for the glory of God's name and the glory of all his virtues.

May we receive this fight and set about it, and persevere in it to the end, in the power of the Lord, in the power of faith. No other weapon strengthens and trains us for this faith than faith alone that Jesus is the Christ. There is no strength in us, or in any creature in heaven and on the earth. But Jesus, the Son of Mary, the Only Begotten of the Father, he is the hero from Judah's line, who conquered the world through his cross! We enter into his work, we rest on his victory, we receive his merits!

Then the victory is ours, because this is the victory that conquers the world—namely, our faith. Many wars have been waged on this earth that, although rightly carried out for freedom and justice, nonetheless ended in defeat and subjection. But here is a fight in which the victory is assured. Christ, elevated to his Father's right hand, is the guarantee of this. He has been anointed King over Zion, God's holy mountain. The nations have been given to him as his inheritance, and the ends of the earth as his possession. Later he will come again in flaming fire, inflicting vengeance on those who do not know God and on those who do not obey the gospel of our Lord Jesus,[32] but also to be glorified in his saints, and to be marveled at among all who have believed.[33] Come, then, Lord Jesus, yes, come quickly!

Amen.

ON PREACHING IN AMERICA[1]

And as regards religious life, it is beyond doubt that [America's moralistic, optimistic, deistic, and experience-led culture] leads to great superficiality. The contrast of sin and grace is weakened. The new birth and the work of the Holy Spirit are shoved into the background. The preaching mostly deals with morals. Election and justification, the entire religious element either falls short or is altogether missing. Preaching is not the unfolding and ministering of the word of God; rather it is a speech, and the text is simply a hook. The religious life, in its entirety, has a different character to our own. Religion does not master the people; the people master religion, just as they also master art and science. Religion is a matter of amusement, of relaxation. The church buildings make this clear. The churches have much that is better than ours: they are cozy [*gezellig*], welcoming, warmed in the winter, without a pulpit; but it is also the case that they could be used as theaters without a single alteration. Light in color, with red carpets, lighthearted, lively, clear, fresh—precisely the opposite of that solemn, dignified, somber, serious [character] found in our European churches. And as the church is, so is the religion. Religion there is an amusement. The preacher is the most in-demand [person], who knows how to speak in the most exciting way (short, varied, lively, theatrical: Rev. Parker,[2] Rev. Pankhurst,[3] Talmage[4]): spirited but shallow, enjoyable, peppered with humor. And this preaching is interspersed with songs, with choirs, with solos, with vocal and instrumental music. Through this, the idea of "church" has almost entirely been lost. Churches are religious societies. Membership by birth and death is not counted. The number of those participating in the Lord's Supper is counted. There are so many sects and unions of churches that the idea of "church" is totally gone. *The* church does not exist there. There is no established church. All [churches] are equal. Individualism thus also reigns on ecclesiastical terrain.

But against this, one can say: what American religious life lacks in depth, it wins in breadth. The distinction between faith and unbelief, as we have here, is unknown there. (We are so astoundingly [focused on] principle that we forget the practice thereof.) There are indeed unbelievers, but they are not organized; they do not make themselves known in their own party. The Democratic and Republican Parties deal with issues wholly outside of belief and unbelief. The fundamental, the spiteful [element] in this battle is lacking. They do not deny each other salvation or heaven. To be against the Anti-Revolutionary Party (against Dr. Kuyper[5]), against Groen,[6] against the free Christian school, here that is taken immediately as opposition to God, Christ, and the Bible. This is not so in America. There are Christians who are Republicans and Christians who are Democrats. There are those who are for, and against, the common school. Some are for, and against, free trade. All of that is outside of "Christian." The "Christian" [approach] is, to a certain extent and in a dualistic manner (theology is not taught at the university; science is separate from faith), next to all the other terrains of this world. All more or less come under the influence of and are shaped by the Christian faith. The state is still vaguely Christian. Prayer remains customary in the primary schools, where the Bible is also still read. The Sabbath and holidays are celebrated nationally and recognized in the busy cities. Days of prayer and thanksgiving are issued by the government. The Columbus Celebration held from 9th–12th October is opened with a demonstration of gratitude in the churches. There is no liberal party that systematically follows the principles of the [French] Revolution and fights against the faith. An orthodox [Christian] is a pariah here, an outsider, unenlightened, but in America this is not so. Gospel preaching on the streets is heard with deep silence. There, one does not think of mockery, of ridicule, such as that of the common riffraff here. The delegates of the Presbyterian Alliance in Toronto[7] were not only received with distinction, they were also hosted by the city mayor and the governor. The interest in churchly and religious matters is exceptional. Sunday schools, home and foreign mission, and all sorts of work in God's kingdom enjoy a level of interest that is unknown here. They are issues alive in the heart and mouth. The meetings of the alliance were attended by great numbers of people for eight days. When mission was dealt with, the speakers had to speak in two churches. And the women's union for mission was attended by a crowd of 1,200 women. It is held as an honor by the richest families if one of their sons becomes a missionary. A very significant lady wished that her only son would dedicate himself to this. Young men and women are no less interested [in mission]. At present there is a union, the Christian Endeavor Society, which began small, but has now spread through the entire English-speaking world and requires its members to be Christian always and everywhere, and to attend the prayer meetings it organizes. The English-speaking world lives for the heathen and sympathizes with its missionaries. It carries the whole heathen world in its heart. Arminianism and Methodism are no less committed in this regard. There is much twaddle in this. But we would do better to carry over the good found therein and to imitate it, than simply to judge everything. The students in particular, in their morality, stand far above those of Europe's universities. This is consistent with the whole principle of formation. The universities are not in the big cities; rather, they are in small, remote places. They form scientific colonies. The students live there in one or more great buildings and are under supervision. A chapel is attached to every school. There is a daily gathering, prayer meeting, the reading of the Bible, singing, prayer, a short address. They are treated as students, not as lords, and receive a particularly practical formation. Religious and moral sensibility is cultivated. Drunkenness and lust are unknown. The manner of living is sober and healthy.

Having seen so much that is good, one shrinks back from critique. May American Christianity develop according to its own law. God has entrusted America with its own high and great calling. [May America] strive for it, in its own way. Calvinism, after all, is not the only truth!

APPENDIX: ON LANGUAGE[1]

It is the privilege of the conscious spiritual life only to be accessible to the subject itself; for who knows a person's thoughts except the spirit of that person, which is in him? (1 Cor. 2:11). The [self-] conscious is a world closed off to others; no one can enter into it without or against that person's will, but God alone (Ps. 139:2). To make himself known to others and to reveal his intimate, hidden life to them, the human being needs a middle. This revelation of the intimate life of the soul can take place in different ways, by different symbols. In general, and in the broadest sense, language is the fullness of the symbols through which a person reveals his thoughts. In this sense there are, thus, as many sorts of languages as there are sorts of symbols. There is a language of signals, by musical instruments, flags, lights, torches; a language of colors and flowers; a language of physiognomy, gestures, movements of muscles, sinews, and bodily parts that are often wholly random, the affections and desires conducting and being a mirror for the inner life of the soul. There is also, finally, a language in sounds that is directed to the ear and that can be articulated or not. The unarticulated language, which is the language of cries, pertains especially to animals. Animals have a unique consciousness, memory, a capacity for appreciation; but their representations remain concrete, detached, and individual. They cannot think in abstraction or form general concepts, and thus they cannot find symbols for these general concepts. This is to say, they cannot bring general concepts to words or names. Language is the Rubicon between the animal and the human.[2]

In the narrower sense, language is the free expression of thought in articulated sounds. It presupposes the higher capacity of knowledge, the reasonable, thinking nature of the human; yes, all the different activities of the human spirit. It presupposes the ability to receive sensations and impressions and to be affected through these. It presupposes the memory, with which we preserve our representations; the imagination, with which we bring our perceptions to life; the understanding, with which we form abstract concepts, and so on. There is an intimate connection between thought (reason) and language. Some people even assert that thinking and speaking are one and the same thing. The so-called Traditionalists, de Bonald,[3] Lamennais,[4] and Bautain,[5] judge that the individual person cannot find higher truths by himself; they must be shared with him externally and that by the word. The person must first hear the word and then he receives the thought. In the same way, a child has no inherent knowledge and does not create language; rather, he receives it from his parents and teachers, and in this language he also receives thoughts and truths, just as Adam listened to God, in order to receive language and his revelation from God. Language is the bearer of truths, the one great and glorious tradition of humankind.[6]

More recently the idea, albeit in another form and for other reasons, that thinking and speaking are one has found acceptance among philosophers. Thinking is, in itself, speaking, speaking is thinking aloud; many people, when thinking, speak out loud. Thinking and speaking, reason and language, belong inseparably to each other. They are identical, two sides of the same coin. Just as there is no concept without words, there are also no words without concepts. Thinking without language is impossible. Logically, the word concerns the thought, language comes before thinking; language was the primary middle in forming the human as a thinking being.[7]

There are many objections, however, to this conflation of thinking and speaking, of reason and language, of concept and word. There is doubtless a close connection between the two, but connection is not the same as identity. The deaf and mute have concepts and thoughts without words; although they have received these concepts and thoughts from others, and although they repeated these in symbols, there is not such a connection between words and concepts that the latter is inseparable from the former. If thinking and speaking were also one, such that the former could not exist without the latter, the appearance of many languages would be inexplicable. The ability to speak is indeed innate, but language is not: we know things and later give this form in different words and languages; the thoughts and concepts are the same, and yet the words are different. The words can even be completely forgotten, and yet the thoughts are preserved and given expression in other symbols; the number five [for example] can be shown by five fingers. Furthermore, we all know from experience that the thoughts within us can exist without words. The thing represented and its symbol are not the same. We often have a representation, a concept, a thought; and we search for the word. It is said of this that if the word is lacking, it is hard for us to recall the thought clearly and plainly. And it is true that the word supports and clarifies the thought, and that one can say something better to the extent that one knows it better; but nonetheless, Augustine says correctly that a human can say nothing that he does not know, but can know something without being able to say it. Our thinking often remains behind the issue [at hand], and our speaking [still further] behind our thinking.[8]

And finally, the indication of a natural link between thinking and speaking is without doubt rightly against the notion that language is artificially invented and exists by appointment and contract. Some names and technical terms may be so viewed, just as musical notes, stenographic symbols, and the hand movements of the deaf and dumb are arbitrarily chosen. But language itself is no product of arbitrariness, convention, and contract. A language invented in this way, for example Volapük,[9] would have no roots in human thought; it would be cut off from all life and poetry and, as such, doomed from the outset. Real, living language is no *Machwerk*.[10] It is a spontaneous, free expression of thought. It is humanity's mark of nobility and the proof and seal of [humanity's] reason. But nonetheless, on the other hand the connection between thought and word is not so close that a particular sound is the physically required, only possible expression of a particular thought. Language did not come into existence by a contract and is not a product of the human will; it is also not a product of nature, growing and withering like a plant. It comes forth from thinking and is thus logical, not physical, in nature. It is not made, but also does not grow like a tree. It is born, as a work of art is born from the soul of the artist. There are thus all sorts of physiological conditions upon which language is dependent, but language itself is nonetheless subject to different laws than those of nature. It has its own nature and character.

The special nature pertaining to language contains some details regarding its origin. The opinion of Locke,[11] Adam Smith,[12] and many others in the previous century that language came into existence by agreement has had its day and now has no representatives. The onomatopoeic inference of language by Herder[13] and Steinthal[14] (the "Bauwau" theory) must encounter the objection that the onomatopoeic words in each language are few and, in addition, unfruitful. The interjectional theory of Condillac[15] (the "Pah-pah" theory) is unacceptable for the same reason: language first begins when interjections stop. Darwinism allows for the development of language from natural cries and does not look for language based on thinking, but rather, asserts thinking from language. There is, however, something to be said against this: natural cries are still not a language and can lead to no language, and the human being did not become human through language, but must have already been human in order to form language. Comparative linguistics teaches, in addition, that the original roots to which language can be retraced were not onomatopoeias, or interjections, or natural cries, or concrete names; rather, they were abstractions. The general came first, and concrete things were named after it. Giving names to things according to their character is the hallmark of humanity.[16] The human being is concerned with language; thinking, anyway, comes before speaking in logical order.

To the extent that it is more deeply researched, nature in this way points to language, just as religion and piety point back to an absolute beginning. The human being is unthinkable without language, even for a single second, and language already presupposes the human. The first human cannot thus have come from an animal: as such, there would thus have been no first human.[17] And he also cannot be considered as a helpless, unemancipated child, because he could not then have lived for a single day without supernatural help. Therefore, the first human must be considered, in accordance with Scripture, as created in adult form, fitted with knowledge and the power of thought. God did not share language with this person externally and mechanically, as the Traditionalists propose. But in the human, created as the image of God, there lay immediately all the abilities and habits that suited him to serve God, to keep his law, to know things, and to name them according to their characters. Why a particular concept was now represented by a particular sound cannot be said with certainty. Max Müller believes that each object makes its own sound; so for example, gold sounds differently from copper; the human, awoken and affected by this (among other things), responded in its own way and had to give an answer (the "Ding-dong" theory). But the appearance of language certainly did not occur so perfectly and instinctively. It cannot be asserted purely on the basis of reactive movements. The original roots are all abstractions and point to thinking, dialogue, and speaking back. Language did not come into existence as φυσις [nature] but as λογῳ [word]. It rests, finally, in the one *Logos* who created all things—spirit and matter, soul and body, subject and object, and also thought and language, concept and word—in connection to each other.[18]

NOTES

INTRODUCTION

1. Herman Bavinck, *Reformed Dogmatics*, ed. John Bolt, trans. John Vriend, 4 vols. (Grand Rapids: Baker, 2003–08).

2. Edward Schillebeeckx, *For the Sake of the Gospel* (New York: Crossroad, 1990), v.

3. Edward Schillebeeckx, *The Collected Works of Edward Schillebeeckx Volume 4: World and Church* (London: T&T Clark, 2014), 31.

4. Bavinck, *Reformed Dogmatics: Prolegomena*, 44.

5. Jan Bavinck, *Een korte schets van mijn leven* (typoscript), 1906, H. Bavinck Archive, no. 346, folder 444 (Amsterdam: Historische Documentatiecentrum), 68. Dutch original: "Er waren drie predikbeurten op den Rustdag des Heeren te vervullen en des winters kwam er nog eene beurt in de week bij."

6. Jan Bavinck, *Een korte schets van mijn leven*, 68. Dutch original: "O ik herinner mij nog levendig enkele beurten, vooral des avonds bij het gaslicht, hoe stil en aandachtig eene groote schare naar de prediking kon luisteren en de woorden van de prediker scheen opte-eten! Er was honger en dorst naar het Woord Gods en de woorden des levens waren spijze en drank voor die hongerige en dorstige zielen. Ik mag gelooven dat mijn arbeid in dit dagen niet zonder vrucht en zegen is geweest."

7. Herman Bavinck, *Dagboek*, 1874. H. Bavinck Archive, no. 346, folder 16 (Amsterdam: Historische Documentatiecentrum), 5 June.

8. Herman Bavinck, *Ex animo et corpore. H. Bavinck, Theol. Stud.*, 1874. H. Bavinck Archive, no. 346, folder 16 (Amsterdam: Historische Documentatiecentrum).

9. J. H. Donner, *Lichtstralen van den kandelaar des woords* (Leiden: D. Donner, 1883). For a selection of Donner's sermons published posthumously, see H. W. Laman, ed., *Wandelen door geloof: overdenkingen*

van de gereformeerde predikanten (Netherlands: Gereformeerd Tractaatgenootschap "Filippus," 1930). For a sermon delivered after the death of Godefridus Johannes Lambertus Berends, a Seceder missionary who had converted from Roman Catholicism, see J. H. Donner, *Afgewezen, maar niet teleurgesteld: Toespraak naar 1 Koningen 8:17–19a* (Kampen: G. Ph. Zalsman, 1873).

10. See, for example, Jan Bavinck, *De zaligheid alleen in den naam van Jezus. Rede ter herdenking van veertigjarige evangelie bediening, uitgesproken 30 September 1888* (Kampen: J. H. Bos, 1888); *Davids bede in den ouderdom. Eene overdenking bij gelegenheid van zijne vijftigjarige bediening van het Woord Gods* (Kampen: G. Ph. Zalsman, 1898); *Feeststoffen* (voor het Kerstfeest en voor het Oud- en Nieuwjaar) (Kampen: G. Ph. Zalsman, 1900); *Feeststoffen* (voor het Paaschfeest) (Kampen: G. Ph. Zalsman, 1901); *De algeheele heiliging van de geloovigen, de wensch van de dienaar des Evangelies.* Afscheidswoord uitgesproken den 25 Januari 1903 (Kampen: J. H. Kok, 1903).

11. Bavinck, *Ex animo et corpore. H. Bavinck, Theol. Stud.*, 18 October 1874.

12. See, for example, J. H. Landwehr, *Prof. Dr. H. Bavinck* (Kampen: J. H. Kok, 1921), 11.

13. Jan de Bruijn and George Harinck, eds., *Een Leidse vriendschap* (Baarn: Ten Have, 1999).

14. Bavinck to Snouck Hurgronje, August 3, 1878, *Een Leidse vriendschap*, 45. Dutch original: "Zondag voor acht dagen heb te Enschede mijn eerste preek gedaan. Ik voor mij had het liever nog was uitgesteld, maar mijn ouders hadden het gaarne en een oom en tante van me, die in Enschede wonen, waren er bijzonder op gesteld. Reeds langen tijd geleden had ik het hun beloofd, daar mijn eerste preek te houden en nu de gezondheidstoestand mijner tante wel van dien aard kon zijn dat ze niet lang meer leefde, was dit redden te meer om mijn belofte te volbrengen. Maar daar was natuurlijk veel bezwaar en met 't oog op ons examen groot tijdverlies aan verbonden. Een preek maken was voor mij geen kleinigheid. Toch lukte het eindelijk. Mijn tekst was 1 Johannes 5:4b, dit is de overwinning die de wereld overwint, namelijk ons geloof. En 't uitspreken viel me zeer mee. Ik was zeer kalm en bedaard. Zoodat ik blij ben dat ik het maar gedaan heb, en de grootste zwarigheid ook hierin weer overwonnen is. Toch was ik in zooverre onvoldaan, dat het mij minder inspireerde dan ik gedacht had. Ik sprak niet met dat gevoel voor mijzelf, als ik gehoopt had dat ik doen zou; terwijl de gedachte, altijd zoo ver beneden 't ideaal te blijven staan, me onophoudelijk bijbleef. Maar overigens ging het goed en heb ik tot dankertekenis overvloedige stof."

15. Bavinck to Snouck Hurgronje, January 6, 1879, in *Een Leidse vriendschap*, 48. Dutch original: "Nu reeds merk ik dat preeken ontzettend veel tijd wegneemt. Eens heb ik hier en eens in Zwolle gesproken. Maar ik weet wel dat, behavle nog één keer in Leiden wat ik beloofd heb, voor mijn doctoraal niet meer aan preeken zal denken." The sermon in Leiden, preached February 29, 1880, was on Gal. 2:20.

16. Herman Bavinck, *Dagboek, 1879–1886*, H. Bavinck Archive, no. 346, folder 16 (Amsterdam: Historische Documentatiecentrum), 25 December 1879.

17. Bavinck to Snouck Hurgronje, January 13, 1881, in *Een Leidse vriendschap*, 81. Dutch original: "Kuenen en Scholten hebben op mij (behalve in de Schriftbeschouwing) niet veel invloed gehad, als ge daaronder verstaat het verliezen van geloofswaarheden en het aannemen van andere, van de hunne. Maar zij hebben wel (hoe kon het anders) invloed gehad op de kracht en de wijze, waarmee ik die waarheden omhels. Het naive van het kinderlijk geloof, van het onbegrensd vertrouwen op de mij ingeprente waarheid, zie, dat ben ik kwijt een dat is veel, heel veel; zoo is die invloed groot en sterk geweest. En nu weet ik wel, dat ik dat nooit terugkrijg. Zelfs vind ik het goed en ben ik er waarlijk en oprecht dankbaar voor, dat ik heb verloren heb. Er was ook in dat naive veel, wat onwaar was en gereinigd moest worden. Maar toch, er is in dat naive (ik week geen beter woord) iets, dat goed is, dat wel doet; iets dat blijven moet, zal de waarheid ons ooit zoet en dierbaar wezen. En als ik dan soms—heel enkel, want och, waar is het rotsensterke geloof van vroeger tijd nog in onse eeuw?—in de gemeente nog enkele menschen ontmoet, die dat hebben en er zoo wel bij zijn en zoo gelukkig, nu, ik kan niet helpen, maar dan wenschte ik weer te gelooven als zij, zoo blij en zoo vrolijk; en dan voel ik, als ik dat had, en ik kon dan zoo preeken, bezield, warm, altijd ten volle overtuigd van wat ik zei, dan kon ik nuttig zijn; zelf levend, zou ik leven voor anderen. Maar ik weet wel, dat is voorbij; dat is thans niet meer mogelijk."

18. Bavinck to Snouck Hurgronje, August 19, 1879, in *Een Leidse vriendschap*, 56–57. Dutch original: "Leiden is me van veelzijdig nut geweest; ik hoop het altijd dankend te erkennen. Maar het heft me ook dikwerf zeer arm gemaakt, me ontnomen, niet alleen veel ballast (daar ben ik blij om) maar ook veel dat ik thans in den lateren tijd, vooral als ik preeken maken moest, als onmisbaar voor eigen geestelijk leven leered beschouwen."

19. See, for example, John Bolt, Editor's Introduction, in Herman Bavinck, *Reformed Dogmatics: Prolegomena* (Grand Rapids: Baker Academic, 2003), 13. The same rendering is also found in John Bolt, *Bavinck*

on the Christian Life: Following Jesus in Faithful Service (Wheaton: Crossway, 2015), 33.

20. Valentijn Hepp, Dr. Herman Bavinck (Amsterdam: W. Ten Have, 1921).

21. Bolt, Editor's Introduction, 12–14; cf. Hepp, Dr. Herman Bavinck, 84.

22. Bolt, Editor's Introduction, 13.

23. James Eglinton, Trinity and Organism: Towards a New Reading of Herman Bavinck's Organic Motif (London: T&T Clark / Bloomsbury, 2012), 27–50.

24. George Harinck, "'Something That Must Remain, If the Truth Is to Be Sweet and Precious to Us': The Reformed Spirituality of Herman Bavinck," Calvin Theological Journal 38 (2003): 252. A more accurate translation is also provided by Willem J. de Wit, "'Will I remain standing?': A Cathartic Reading of Herman Bavinck," The Bavinck Review 2 (2011): 25.

25. R. Bremmer, Herman Bavinck en zijn tijdgenoten (Kampen: Kok, 1966), 35.

26. Bremmer, Herman Bavinck en zijn tijdgenoten, 35.

27. Bavinck to Snouck Hurgronje, June 16, 1881, in Een Leidse vriendschap, 86–87. Dutch original: "Als ge eens bedenkt, dat ik elken zondag twee keer preeken moet, vier catechisantiën 's weeks heb te houden, verden aan huis- en ziekenbezoek veel tijd moet wijden en dan soms nog een Friesche begrafenis heb te leiden, dan behoeft ge niet meer te vragen, of er voor eigen studie veel tijd en gelegenheid overblijft."

28. Herman Bavinck, Dagboek, March 20, 1881. Dutch original: "In Franeker gepreekt over Jesaia 53:4–6 en Catech. Vraag 1 (voor 't eerst geheel geimproviseerd, ging goed)."

29. Bavinck to Snouck Hurgronje, June 16, 1881, in Een Leidse vriendschap, 87. Dutch original: "Wat mij 't moeilijkst in mijn werk valt, is om mij altijd op te heffen tot en te blijven op de ideale hoogte van mijn geloof en belijdenis. O, altijd met het heliege te moeten omgaan, steeds tot gebed of tot dankzegging, tot vermaning of vertroosting geroepen te worden, en dan dikwerf zoo weinig zelf in die telkens wisselende toestanden te kunnen inleven, dat valt hard, kweekt een gevoel van onvoldaanheid en dikwerf van onverschilligheid. Ik begrijp het thans nog beter als vroeger, hoe onder het gewaad van den geestelijke een diep-onheilig, gevoelloos en huichelachtig hart wonen kan. Behalve dit erniste en drukkende bezwaar

van het predikantambt, is er nog een schaduwzijde aan verbonden, die ik ook diep gevoel, en dat is, dat men altijd 'dominé' is een nooit eens recht vertrouwelijk meer spreken kan. Althans zoo gaat het mij. Tot dusver heb ik hier nog niemand gevonden, wien ik dat vertrouwen mag en durf schenken. En dat valt me hard. Thuis ben ik alleen, op mijn kamer, en buiten ben ik altijd de 'dominé'. Zoo ooit, dan heb ik in den laatsten tijd verlangd naar eene vrouw, die mij begrijpen en aan wie ik mij gansch en al toevertrouwen kan."

30. Bavinck to Snouck Hurgronje, September 23, 1881, in *Een Leidse vriendschap*, 92. Dutch original: "Maar ondankbaar mag ik toch niet wezen. 't Gaat mij tot dusverre goed, beter dan ik durfde denken en verwachten. Mijne prediking blijft niet zonder vrucht. De liefde der gemeente valt mij ruimschoots ten deel."

31. Bavinck to Snouck Hurgronje, March 7, 1882, in *Een Leidse vriendschap*, 95. Dutch original: "Ik troost me hiermee, dat ik in mijn predikantsbetrekking niet ongezegend arbeid. Als er van die oude vromen tot mij komen, die me zeggen, hoe ze door door mijn woord gesterkt en vertroost zijn, of anderen, die nu een gansch ander leven kennen en leiden—dan is me dat tot bemoediging en ik ontvang dan den indruk, dat ik toch niet gansch nutteloos op aarde geleef heb en leef. En zulke ogenblikken zijn dan onbetaalbaar en kunnen door niets anders verged worden."

32. Bremmer, *Herman Bavinck en zijn tijdgenoten*, 39.

33. Bremmer, *Herman Bavinck en zijn tijdgenoten*, 43.

34. Bavinck, *Dagboek*, August 24, 1882. Dutch original: "Treffend ogenblik voor mij en mijn vader."

35. Jan Bavinck, *Een korte schets van mijn leven*, 69.

36. Herman Bavinck, *De Welsprekendheid: Eene Lezing* (Kampen: G. Ph. Zalsman, 1901).

37. Herman Bavinck, *De Wereldverwinnende Kracht des Geloofs: Leerrede over 1 Joh. 5:4b, uitgesproken in de Burgwalkerk te Kampen den 30sten Juni 1901* (Kampen: G. Ph. Zalsman, 1901). Dutch original: "Deze leerrede word uitgesproken bij gelegenheid, dat President Kruger met zijn gevolg, tijdens zijn bezoek aan Kampen, op Zondag 30 Juni 1901 in de vergadering der gemeente tegenwoordig was. Velen, die ze hoorden, gaven het verlangen te kennen, dat ze in druk verschijnen mocht. Hoewel ik ze niet letterlijk weergeven kon, maakte ik toch geen bezwaar, om aan dat vriendelijk verzoek te voldoen. Zakelijk komt ze geheel met het toen gesproken woord overeen."

38. Herman Bavinck, *Philosophy of Revelation* (New York: Longmans, Green, and Co., 1909).

39. Abraham Kuyper, *Lectures on Calvinism* (Grand Rapids: Eerdmans, 1931).

40. Hepp, *Dr. Herman Bavinck*, 303.

41. Hepp, *Dr. Herman Bavinck*, 304.

BAVINCK'S FOREWORD TO *ELOQUENCE*

1. C. H. Spurgeon, "Preaching for the Poor," sermon delivered on Sunday, January 25, 1857.

2. Here, Bavinck cites Schleiermacher's "On the Social Element of Religion" (1711). English translation from Frederic Henry Hedge, *Prose Writers of Germany* (New York: C. S. Francis and Company, 1855), 443.

3. 2 Cor. 11:2.

ELOQUENCE

1. Herman Bavinck, *De Welsprekendheid: Eene Lezing* (Kampen: Zalsman, 1901). This booklet was originally a lecture given to the students of the Theological School in Kampen on November 28, 1889.

2. Col. 4:6.

3. John 1:1.

4. English translation by Gary Bachlund, "Zest for Life" (1989).

> Wenn im Unendlichen Dasselbe
> Sich wiederholend ewig fliesst,
> Das tausendfältige Gewölbe
> Sich kräftig in einander schliesst;
> Strömt Lebenslust aus allen Dingen,
> Dem kleinsten wie dem grössten Stern,
> Und alles Drängen, alles Ringen
> Ist ew'ge Ruh in Gott dem Herrn.

5. Homer, *Iliad*, Book 1.

6. 1 Cor. 14:10.

7. Willem Bilderdijk (1756–1831), a Dutch Calvinist poet. See also Herman Bavinck, *Bilderdijk als denker en dichter* (Kampen: J. H. Kok, 1906).

8. Willem Bilderdijk, *De Dieren: Dichtstuk* (Amsterdam: P. den Hengst en Zoon, 1817), 19–20.

> O, vloeibre klanken, waar, met d'adem uitgegoten,
> De ziel (als Godlijk licht, in stralen afgeschoten)
> Zichzelve in meedeelt ! meer dan licht of melody;
> Maar schepsel van 't gevoel in de engste harmony,
> Die 't stofloos met het stof verenigt en vermengelt!
> Door wie zich 't hart ontlast, verademt en verengelt!

9. Here, Bavinck cites Bilderdijk's poem "De Taal" ("Speech"), *Krekelzangen*, Eerste Deel (Rotterdam: J. Immerzeel Junior, 1822), 97. In line two of the section cited below, Bavinck writes of "truth" in the lower case (*waarheid*). Bilderdijk's original capitalizes this as "Truth" (*Waarheid*) and is likely a reference to Jesus Christ as "the Truth" (cf. John 14:6).

> Dan Platoos school, dan heel Atheen bevatten;
>   Houdt waarheid ja, en echten hemelzin
> En 't begrip der ons verleende schatten.
> Ken starveling, ken geheel uw ziel in haar!
>   Zij maakt u mensch; in haar berust uw wezen.
> Neem in uw sprak uw eigen zelfheid waar;
>   Leer daar uzelf, leer daar uw God in lezen!

10. Here, Bavinck cites the following lines of Bilderlijk's poem "De Dieren" cited earlier. See footnote 7.

> Maar goodelijke gift, met d'ademtocht van 't leven
> Aan 't schepsel ingestort, zoover er geesten zweven,
> (Is ze tevens) met zijn val, vervallen en ontaard.

11. "Hinc discidium illud exstitit quasi linguae atque cordis absurdum sane et inutile et reprehendendum." Cicero, *de Oratore* III 16, 61. "This is the source from which has sprung the undoubtedly absurd, unprofitable and reprehensible language of the heart."

12. Charles Maurice de Talleyrand-Périgord (1754–1838), a French diplomat.

13. "La parole a été donné à l'homme pour déguiser sa pensée."

14. English translation from John Bowring, *Sketch of the Language and Literature of Holland* (Amsterdam: Diederichs Brothers, 1829), 11–12.

> Maar weg met u, o spraak van basterklanken
> Waarin hyeen en valsche schakels janken;
> Verlooch'nares van afkomst en geslacht,
> Gevormd voor spot, die met de waarheid lacht;
> Wier staamlarij, bij eeuwig woordverbreken,
> In 't neusgehuil, zichzelf niet uit durft spreken.
> Verfoeilijk fransch, alleen den duivel waard,
> Die met uw aapgegrijns zich meester maakt van de aard!

15. "Zoek daarom de welsprekendheid niet bij de Jansalie-naturen, bij de handelaars in verdraagzaamheid en neutraliteit." Bavinck, *De Welsprekendheid*, 24. The mention of Jan Salie (John Sage) refers to the personification of the nineteenth-century Dutch spirit as sluggish and inert, as found in the writings of Everhardus Potgieter. In that context, the herb sage (Dutch: *salie*) was viewed as sleep-inducing. See E. J. Potgieter, *Proza 1835–1847*, in E. J. Potgieter, *De werken*, Deel I, ed. J. C. Zimmerman (Haarlem: H. D. Tjeenk Willink, 1908).

16. Here, Bavinck refers to the Muses, the goddesses of literature, science, and the arts in classical Greek literature. See Jean-Luc Nancy, *Les Muses* (Paris: Editions Galilée, 1994).

17. John Calvin, *Lettres françaises*, ed. J. Bonnet, 2 vols. (Paris: Mayrueis, 1854), 1:114, April 28, 1545.

18. Multatuli (from the Latin *multa tuli*, "I have carried much") was the penname of Eduard Douwes Dekker (1820–87), a Dutch atheistic satirical author. Abraham Kuyper referred to Nietzsche as the "German Multatuli." See Abraham Kuyper, "The Blurring of the Boundaries," in *Abraham Kuyper: A Centennial Reader*, ed. James Bratt (Grand Rapids: Eerdmans, 1998), 364. "Today our neighbors to the east have their own Multatuli in Friedrich Nietzsche."

19. Multatuli's best-known work is his novel *Max Havelaar, of de koffie-veilingen der Nederlandsche Handel-Maatschappy* [*Max Havelaar: Or the Coffee Auctions of the Dutch Trading Company*]. Amsterdam: De Ruyter, 1860. In this book, the central character, Max Havelaar, works against corruption in the then Dutch East Indies.

20. Batavius Droogstoppels, a coffee merchant, and Slijmeringen, his business partner, in *Max Havelaar*. Droogstoppels is a caricature of the typical Dutch businessman of that era.

21. Multatuli, *Max Havelaar*, ch. 11.

22. 2 Cor. 4:13.

23. Luke 19:40.

24. Jer. 20:9.

25. Amos 3:8.

26. John 12:49.

27. This statement is taken from Ovid's *Fasti* 6.5–8:

> est Deus in nobis; agitante calescimus illio:
> impetus hic sacrae semina mentis habet.
> fas mihi praecipue voltus vidisse deorum
> vel quia sum vates, vel quia sacra cano.

Bavinck also uses the same quotation in "Of Beauty and Aesthetics," *Essays on Religion, Science, and Society*, ed. John Bolt, trans. Harry Boonstra and Gerrit Sheeres (Grand Rapids: Baker, 2008), 252. This statement is also quoted elsewhere by Abraham Kuyper in a lecture to students at the Free University of Amsterdam in 1890. See Abraham Kuyper, *Scholarship: Two Convocational Addresses on University Life* (Grand Rapids: Christian's Library Press, 2014), 28.

28. Johannes Matthias Schrant (1783–1866), a Dutch theologian, rhetorician, and literary scholar.

29. Friedrich Rückert (1788–1866) was a German poet.

30. Friedrich Rückert, *Die Weisheit des Brahmannen: ein Lehrgedicht in Bruchstücken*, vol. 4 (Leipzig: Weidmann, 1841), 254.

> Est is ein wahres Wort, der Künstler wird geboren,
> Doch jede Wahrheit wirt Irrthum im Munde der Thoren.
> Geboren wird mit ihm der Kunsttrieb, nicht die Kunst,
> Die Bildung ist sein Werk, die Anlag' Himmelsgunst.

31. "Semper statui, neminem sapientiae laudem et eloquentiae sine summon studio et labore et doctrina consequi posse." Cicero, *de Orat.* II, 89. "Multo labore, assiduo studio, varia exercitatione, plurimis experimentis, altissima prudential, praesentissimo consilio constat ars dicendi." Quintilian, *Orat. Instit.* II, 13.

32. "Scio quaeri etiam, natura plus ad eloquentiam conferat an doctrina. Consummatus orator nisi ex utraque fieri potest. Si parti utrilibet omnino alteram detrahes, natura etiam sine doctrina multum valebit, doctrina nulla esse sine natura poterit." Quintilian, t.a.p. II, 19.

33. Luke 6:45.

34. François Fénélon (1651–1715), a French Roman Catholic theologian.

35. Arthur Schopenhauer (1788–1860), a German philosopher.

36. Here, Bavinck refers to the Rev. Zielknyper ("Rev. Psychiatrist"), a character in Multatuli's *Ideeën*, who follows a liturgy obviously parodying that of the Dutch Reformed Church, but which is directed to "the NANNY" (*de BAKER*) rather than "the LORD" (*de HEER*). Multatuli, *Ideeën I* (Amsterdam: Funke, 1879), 297–305.

37. John 12:49.

38. This and others, also some later examples, can be found in Jan Hartog, *Geschiedenis der Predikkunde en de evangelieprediking: in de protestantsche kerk van Nederland* (Amsterdam: Frederik Muller, 1861); and Sincerus, *De Kanselontluistering in de Ned. Herv. Kerk tijdens de 17de en 18de eeuw aangewezen en gestaafd* (Amsterdam: 1852).

39. Nicholaas Beets (1814–1903), a Dutch author, poet, and preacher who wrote under the pseudonym "Hildebrand."

40. "Hij die de kennis zoekt en wijsheid niet daarbij, vrijt naar de kamenier en gaat de vrouw voorbij."

41. Compare with Martin Luther, *Martin Luther's Tabletalk*, ed. William Hazlitt (Fearn, Scotland, UK: Christian Focus Publications, 2003), 276–77. "I would not have preachers in their sermons use Hebrew, Greek, or foreign languages, for in the church we ought to speak as we used to do at home, the plain mother tongue, which everyone is acquainted with. It may be allowed in courtiers, lawyers, advocates, etc., to use quaint, curious words. Doctor Staupitz is a very learned man, yet he is a very irksome preacher; and the people had rather hear a plain brother preach, that delivers his words simply to their understanding. In churches no praising or extolling should be sought after. St. Paul never used such high and stately words as Demosthenes and Cicero did, but he spake, properly and plainly, words which signified and showed high and stately matters, and he did well."

42. Bavinck's precise meaning in this sentence is unclear. "En dat kan de Evangelie-prediker te beter doen, wijl in het Christendom alles concreet, aanschouwlijk, persoonlijk, of wilt gij den diepsten grond, wijl het trinitarisch is." *De Welsprekendheid*, 42–43. He maintains that the sermon must be rich and deep by way of content, but it must not limit itself to abstract or dogmatic reflection: it must illustrate and narrate, rather than simply describe.

43. Cf. Herman Bavinck, *Reformed Dogmatics: Prolegomena*, ed. John Bolt, trans. John Vriend (Grand Rapids: Baker, 2003), 383. "In Christ, in

the middle of history, God created an organic centre; from this centre, in an ever widening sphere, God drew circles within which the light of revelation shines. . . . Presently the grace of God appears to all human beings. The Holy Spirit takes everything from Christ, adding nothing new to revelation. . . . In Christ God both fully revealed and fully gave himself. Consequently also Scripture is complete; it is the perfected Word of God."

44. This most likely refers to the Japhetic theory of Nicholas Yakovlevich Marr (1865–1934), who argued that the Kartvelian and Semitic languages were related, a theory that gained popularity among Soviet linguists. W. K. Matthews, "The Japhetic Theory," *The Slavonic and East European Review* 27, no. 68 (December 1948): 172–92. Cf. Herman Bavinck, *Reformed Dogmatics: Holy Spirit, Church and New Creation*, ed. John Bolt, trans. John Vriend (Grand Rapids: Baker, 2008), 661. "All Old Testament concepts shed their external, national-Israelitish meanings and become manifest in their spiritual and eternal sense. The Semitic no longer needs to be transposed into the Japhetic, as Bunsen wished, for the New Testament itself has given to the particularistic ideas of the Old Testament a universal and cosmic meaning."

45. This is taken from Bilderdijk's poem, "Aan de verbeelding" (1818):

> Verbeelding, welige aâr, en vruchtbre moederschoot,
> Uit Wien, door 't hart bevrucht, een nieuw heelal ontsproot,
> Waarin, op vleuglen van zijn almacht rondgedragen,
> De dichtgeest zwiert en zweeft met Godlijk zelfbehagen
> En warelden vol glans hervoort roept.

The version cited by Bavinck differs slightly:

> Waarin op vleuglen van zijn almacht rondgedragen,
> De Dichtkunst zwiert en zweeft met Godlijk zelfbehagen,
> En warelden vol glans hervoort roept uit haar graf.

46. Ons zegen Vader ende Soon,
>   Ons zegen d'Heijlige Geest,
>   Dien al de wereld eer betoon,
>   Voor Hem hun verse meeste.

47. Liefste Jesu, wij zijn hier
>   U en Uw woord aan te horen;
>   Onze zinnen so bestier,
>   Dat zijn kragt niet gaa verloren
>   Maar ons hart daarvoor bewogen
>   Tot u werde opgetoen! Amen.

48. De Godsvrucht zweeg en gaf een kus
    Uit eerbeid aan Velingius.

49. This is a poetic citation of Num. 15:12.

50. Jan Vos (1612–67), a Dutch poet.

51. Emile Zola (1840–1902), a French writer central to the development
of theatrical naturalism.

52. Houdt aller harten in uw handen!
    Doorwoelt, doorwroet onze ingewanden!
    Beheerscht verbeelding en verstand!
    Kneed, kneed onze inborst met uw vingren!
    Leert van Jupijn den bliksem slingeren!
    Maar zet er zielen mee in brand!
    't Gemeen moog' vruchtloos naar den hoogen
    U starend trachten na te oogen
    't Gevoele u in 't geschokte hart!
    Het ween, het lach, het gloei, het ijze,
    Naar dat uw zangtoon dale of rijze,
    Of zink' in onbeweegbre smart.
    Het haat', het minn', het zet zich open,
    Het krimp' naar 't onweerstaanbre nopen
    Der geesel, daar uw hand mee zweept,
    En heb gevoel, noch wil, noch leven,
    Dan die 't uw zangtoon weet te geven,
    Die 't in zijn golving medesleept.

53. Herman Witsius (1636–1708), a Dutch theologian.

54. Jan War preekt roerend, zegt gij. Kom,

    Ik wil het ook gelooven.
    Hij roert een pot met woorden om,
    En hutst het onderst boven.

55. 2 Cor. 5:20.

56. "Oratorem nisi qui sapiens esset esse neminem, atque ipsam eloquentiam, quod ex bene dicendi scientia constaret, unam quondam esse
virtutem et qui unam virtutem haberet omnes habere," Cicero, de Orat.,
I. 18. "Neque tantum id dico, eum qui sit orator, virum bonum esse
oportere, sed ne futurum quidem oratorem, nisi virum bonnum. . . .
Non igitur unquam malus idem homo et perfectus orator." Quintilianus,
Instit. XII, 1.

57. Ludwig Friedrich Franz Theremin (1780–1846), a German Protestant theologian.

58. Christian Johann Heinrich Heine (1797–1856), a German poet, essayist, and satirist.

59. Jean-Jacques Rousseau, "La Confession de foi du vicaiare Savoyard," in *Oeuvres complètes de J.J. Rousseau: Emile, Tome II* (Paris: Dupont, 1823), 14–207.

60. Hugues-Félicité Robert de Lamennais, *Paroles d'un croyant* (Paris: Bibliotheque Nationale, 1897).

61. Jean-Baptiste Massillon (1663–1742), a French Roman Catholic Bishop.

62. Here, Bavinck draws his citation from J. Schade's Dutch translation of Franz Theremin's original German text *Demosthenes und Massillon* (Berlin: Duncker und Humbolt, 1845). See Franz Theremin, *Demosthenes en Massillon: Eene Bijdrage Tot de Geschiedenis der Welsprekendheid*, trans. J. Schade ('s-Gravenhage: J. M. van 't Haaff, 1847), 165.

63. Herman Agatho des Amorie van der Hoeven (1829–97), a Dutch jurist.

64. Petrus Augustus de Génestet (1829–61), a Dutch theologian and poet.

65. Nicholaas Beets, *De Gedichten van Nicholaas Beets* (Gent: H. Hoste, 1848), 98.

Laat schooner verzen glad van effen lippen vloeien,
Maar gil noch galm noch kwaak noch bulder, woest en luid,
Weerhoud uw arm en hand van haamren, zwaaien, roeien,
De molenwiekerij drukt geen verrukking uit.

66. Here, Bavinck adds in a footnote, "Happily, in this regard it seems that in recent years a marked improvement has been seen."

67. Gij prediker daar hoog in de lucht,
Hebt gij dan geen woordje voor mij?
Uw rede als een galmend gerucht,
Rolt ledig mijn ziele voorbij.

68. Phil. 4:8.

69. Matt. 7:16.

70. Johann Paul Friedrich Richter (1763–1825), a German Romantic writer.

71. Bavinck cites Bilderdijk's poem "Het Buitenleven" (1802). See J. van Vloten, *Nederlandsch Dicht en Ondicht der Negentiende Eeuw* (Deventer: A. ter Gunne, 1861), 82.

Gij dichter, bezig alwat geest en kunst gehengen,
Leer 't aaklige aan het blijde, en 't sterke aan 't zachte mengen,
En stem uw tonen naar het voorwerp, dat gij malt,
Dat zelfs de klank van 't vers uw denkbeeld achterhaalt.

Laat Zefir in uw zang op luchte vlerkjes zuizen,
En 't kabblend nat der beek met zacht gemurmel bruizen,
Doch stort zich 't stroomend nat met zieded buldren uit,
Zoo siddre uw woest muzyk van 't dondrend stoomgeluid.

Laat d' os, in 't juk gebukt, den harden kleigrond ploegen;
Men voele in 't moede dier, en long en boezem zwoegen,
En 't traag en worstlend vers ga dof en langzaam voort,
Als wierd zijn logge stap op elken plof gehoord.

De vlugge hinde vlie door de onafzienbre dalen;
Men volge in bliksemvlucht en wete ze in te halen,
En schoeie 't luchtig vers gezwinde wieken aan!

Gelukkig, zoo de taal uw poging bij wil staan,
En geen beperkte keus van maat en lettergrepen
U eeuwig in 't geklep des rijmvals meê blijft slepen!
Bataven, kent uw spraak en heel haar overvloed;
Zijt meester van de taal, gij zijt het van 't gemoed!

72. The Dutch proverb "Wie geeft wat hij heeft, is waard dat hij leeft" means that only by giving one's all can one be beyond reproach.

73. Horace, *Odes* III.i.

74. Favorinus of Arelate (ca. AD 80–160), a Roman sophist and philosopher.

75. "Accedat oportet actio varia, vehemens, plena animi, plena spiritus, plena doloris, plena veritatis." Cicero, *de Orat.* II, 17.

76. "Animi est omnis action, et imago animi vultus est, indices oculi." Cicero, *de Orat.* III, 59.

77. Louis Bourdaloue (1632–1704), a French Jesuit known as "the blind preacher" for his habit of preaching with his eyes closed.

78. Matthias Claudius (1740–1815), a German poet who wrote under the pen name "Asmus."

79. Allard Pierson (1831–96), a Dutch theologian.

80. Nikolaus Franz Niembsch Edler von Strehlenau (1802–50), an Austrian poet who wrote under the pen name "Nikolaus Lenau."

81. Die Künste der Hellenen kannten
    Nicht den Erlöser und sein Licht,
    D'rum scherzten sie so gern und nannten
    Des Schmerzes tiefsten Abgrund nicht.

    Dass sie am Schmerz, den sie zu trösten
    Nicht wusste, mild vorüber führt,
    Erkenn' ich als der Zauber grössten
    Womit uns die Antike rührt.

82. John 18:38.

THE SERMON AND THE SERVICE

1. This piece was originally written by Bavinck as "De Predikdienst," in *De Vrije Kerk* no. 1, IX (January 1883): 32–43, and was later included in Herman Bavinck, *Kennis en Leven* (Kampen: J. H. Kok, 1922), 78–85.

2. Jan van Andel (1839–1910), a minister in Bavinck's denomination.

3. Rom. 10:7.

4. Phil. 3:10.

5. In Bavinck's context, the term "motto-preaching" (*motto-preeken*) caricatured the practice of using a biblical text as a hook (or motto) from which the content of the sermon would hang tenuously. See, for example, Johannes Jacobus van Oosterzee, *Johannes Jacobus. Practische theologie: een handboek voor jeugdige godgeleerden*, Deel 1 (Utrecht: Kemink, 1877).

6. 1 Cor. 2:4.

7. Isa. 55:11.

8. This refers to the magazine *The Free Church* (*De Vrije Kerk*) in which Bavinck was writing.

THE WORLD-CONQUERING POWER OF FAITH

1. Herman Bavinck, *De Wereldverwinnende Kracht des Geloofs: Leerrede over 1 Joh. 5:4b, uitgesproken in de Burgwalkerk te Kampen den 30sten Juni 1901* (Kampen: P. H. Zalsman, 1901). An alternative translation of this sermon has also been printed in Bolt, *Bavinck on the Christian Life*, 235–52. These translations were produced independently, simultaneously, and unbeknownst to either translator. My translation is included in this book for the sake of completeness.

2. Stephanus Johannes Paulus Kruger (1825–1904), more commonly known as Paul Kruger, was president of the South African Republic (Transvaal) and the face of Afrikaner resistance against the British during the Second Boer War (1899–1902). For an autobiographical memoir of Kruger's visit to Kampen, see Paul Kruger, *The Memoirs of Paul Kruger: Four Times President of the South African Republic*, vol. 2 (London: T. Fisher Unwin, 1902), 371. "I also revisited Kampen, the Mecca of the Protestant Church . . . my reception was of the most cordial nature imaginable."

3. "Unbelief and Revolution" was the title of the Anti-Revolutionary statesman Groen van Prinsterer's most significant work. Guillaume Groen van Prinsterer, *Ongeloof en revolutie. Eene reeks van historische voorlezingen* (Leiden: S. and J. Luchtmans, 1847). Published in English as *Groen van Prinsterer's Lectures on Unbelief and Revolution*, trans. Harry van Dyke (Jordan Station, Canada: Wedge Publishing Foundation, 1989).

4. Here, Bavinck refers to the Boer Wars, fought in South Africa (1880–81 and 1899–1902) between the British Empire and two independent Boer states, the Orange Free State and the Transvaal Republic.

5. This refers to the 1901 election, in which the Anti-Revolutionary Party, led by the Reformed theologian Abraham Kuyper, came a very close second to the Liberal Party. Kuyper was asked to form a coalition government and became prime minister that August.

6. Ps. 65:11b.

7. Ps. 8:5.

8. An orrery is a moving model of the solar system and corresponds to Bavinck's original Dutch phrase, "het raderwerk der schepping Gods."

9. 1 John 2:16.

10. John 8:34.

11. 2 Kings 5:12.

12. Heb. 11:7.

13. Heb. 11:8.

14. Heb. 11:24–26.

15. Heb. 11:29–30.

16. Heb. 11:33–34.

17. Isa. 53:2.

18. Rom. 9:5.

19. Heb. 11:3.

20. Rom. 8:31.

21. Ps. 118:14–16.

22. Rom. 8:33.

23. Rom. 8:34–35, 37.

24. 1 Cor. 2:4.

25. For the particular history of this sentiment in the context of the Dutch Reformation, see Carter Lindberg, "The Blood of the Martyrs: The Reformation in the Netherlands," in *The European Reformations* (Oxford: Wiley Blackwell, 2010), 282–92.

26. 1 John 4:8.

27. John 16:33.

28. Eph. 6:14, 16–17.

29. 2 Cor. 13:5.

30. James 4:4.

31. 1 John 2:16.

32. 2 Thess. 1:8.

33. 2 Thess. 1:10.

ON PREACHING IN AMERICA

1. Excerpted from Herman Bavinck, "Mijne reis naar Amerika" (unpublished, H. Bavinck Archive, no. 346, box 64). The book was later published as *Mijne reis naar Amerika*, ed. George Harinck (Barneveld: Uitgeverij Vuurbaak, 1998). An English translation of *Mijne reis naar*

Amerika was published as "My Journey to America," ed. George Harinck, trans. James Eglinton, *Dutch Crossing: Journal of Low Countries Studies* 41:2 (2017): 180–93.

2. Joel Parker (1799–1873), a Presbyterian pastor and celebrated revivalist preacher in New York.

3. Charles Henry Pankhurst (1842–1933), a Presbyterian pastor and social reformer. He rose to prominence in New York after preaching against the corruption of the police there in 1892.

4. Thomas De Witt Talmage (1832–1902), a renowned Presbyterian pastor in New York.

5. Abraham Kuyper (1837–1920), the leader of the Anti-Revolutionary Party, founder of the Vrije Universiteit Amsterdam, and a Reformed pastor.

6. Guillaume Groen van Prinsterer (1801–76), a jurist and classicist, statesman and publicist. He was the father of the Anti-Revolutionary movement in the Netherlands.

7. In his visit to North America, Bavinck also traveled to Canada.

APPENDIX: ON LANGUAGE

1. This was originally the section titled "De taal," in Herman Bavinck, *Beginselen der psychologie* (Kampen: J. H. Bos, 1897), 120–25. Although it does not deal with preaching directly, this text is nonetheless useful as a supplementary reading to Bavinck's *Eloquence*.

2. Max Müller, *Vorlesungen über die Wissenschaft der Sprache*, I Serie, 3rd ed. (Leipzig: J. Klinkhardt, 1875), S. 16, 416, 421. See also Herman Bavinck, *Reformed Dogmatics: Prolegomena*, ed. John Bolt, trans. John Vriend (Grand Rapids: Baker Academic, 2003), 377.

3. Louis Gabriel Ambroise, Vicomte de Bonald (1754–1840), a French counterrevolutionary writer from the Traditionalist school. De Bonald argued, "*L'homme pense sa parole avant de parler sa pensée*" ("A man thinks his word before speaking his thought").

4. Hugues-Félicité Robert de Lamennais (1782–1854), a French Catholic priest and philosopher.

5. Louis Eugène Marie Bautain (1796–1867), a French theologian and philosopher.

6. Albert Stöckl, *Lehrbuch der Philosophie*, 6th ed. I (Mainz: F. Kirchheim, 1887), S. 406; Paul Janet, *Traité élémentaire de philosophie: à l'usage des classes* (Paris: Delagrave, 1889).

7. Max Müller, *Das Denken im Lichte der Sprache* (Leipzig: Engelmann, 1888), S. 70–115.

8. Compare Theodor Gangauf, *Des h. Augustinus speculative Lehre von Gott dem Dreieinigen* (Augsburg: Schmidt, 1883), S. 138–40. Additionally, regarding the connection between thinking and speaking, Benno Erdmann, *Die psychol. Grundlagen der Beziehung zw. Sprechen und Denken.* Archiv für systemat. Philos. herausg. Von Natorp. Neue Folge der Philos. Monatshefte II (1896), S. 355–56 (1897), S. 31–32, 150–51, Friedrich Jodl, *Lehrbuch der Psychologie* (Stuttgart: J. G. Cotta'sche Buchhandlung Nachfolger GmbH., 1903), 564–65.

9. Volapük is an auxiliary language created 1879–80 by Johann Martin Schleyer, a German Roman Catholic priest who claimed God had instructed him to create an international language. At present, it is estimated to have approximately twenty speakers. See Johann Martin Schleyer, Alfred Kirchhoff, Klas August Linderfelt, *Volapük: Easy Method of Acquiring the Universal Language* (C. N. Caspar, 1888).

10. Here, Bavinck uses the German term *Machwerk*, which has no direct Dutch (or English) equivalent. It denotes a large object produced artificially and lacking in quality.

11. John Locke (1632–1704), an English philosopher generally regarded as the father of classical liberalism.

12. Adam Smith (1723–90), a Scottish moral philosopher.

13. Johann Gottfried von Herder (1744–1803), a German philosopher. Herder argued that language determines thought.

14. Hermann Steinthal (1823–99), a German philologist.

15. Étienne Bonnot de Condillac (1714–80), a French philosopher.

16. Max Müller, *Vorlesungen über die Wissenschaft der Sprache* I, 425–26.

17. The meaning of this sentence is that had the first human come from animal, it would have remained an animal, rather than become a human.

18. Regarding the origin of language, compare Max Müller, *Vorlesungen über die Wissenschaft der Sprache* I, 408–68; and Alexander Giesswein, *Die Hauptprobleme der Sprachwissenschaft* (Freiburg: Herder, 1892), S. 140–41.

BIBLIOGRAPHY

Bavinck, Herman. *Beginselen der psychologie*. Kampen: J. H. Bos, 1897.

——. *Bilderdijk als denker en dichter*. Kampen: J. H. Kok, 1906.

——. *Dagboek*, 1874. H. Bavinck Archive, no. 346, folder 16. Amsterdam: Historische Documentatiecentrum.

——. "De Predikdienst." In *De Vrije Kerk* no. 1, IX (January 1883): 32–43.

——. *De Welsprekendheid: Eene Lezing*. Kampen: G. Ph. Zalsman, 1901.

——. *De Wereldverwinnende Kracht des Geloofs: Leerrede over 1 Joh. 5:4b, uitgesproken in de Burgwalkerk te Kampen den 30sten Juni 1901*. Kampen: Ph. Zalsman, 1901.

——. *Ex animo et corpore. H. Bavinck, Theol. Stud.*, 1874. H. Bavinck Archive, no. 346, folder 16. Amsterdam: Historische Documentatiecentrum.

——. *Mijne reis naar Amerika*. Edited by George Harinck. Barneveld: Uitgeverij Vuurbaak, 1998.

——. "My Journey to America." Edited by George Harinck. Translated by James Eglinton. *Dutch Crossing: Journal of Low Countries Studies* 41:2 (2017): 180–93.

——. "Of Beauty and Aesthetics." In *Essays on Religion, Science, and Society*, 245–60, edited by John Bolt, translated by Harry Boonstra and Gerrit Sheeres. Grand Rapids: Baker, 2008.

——. *Philosophy of Revelation*. New York: Longmans, Green, and Co., 1909.

——. *Reformed Dogmatics*. Edited by John Bolt. Translated by John Vriend. 4 vols. Grand Rapids: Baker, 2003–2008.

Bavinck, Jan. *Davids bede in den ouderdom. Eene overdenking bij gelegenheid van zijne vijftigjarige bediening van het Woord Gods.* Kampen: Ph. Zalsman, 1898.

———. *De algeheele heiliging van de geloovigen, de wensch van de dienaar des Evangelies.* Afscheidswoord uitgesproken den 25 Januari 1903. Kampen: J. H. Kok, 1903.

———. *De zaligheid alleen in den naam van Jezus. Rede ter herdenking van veertigjarige evangelie bediening, uitgesproken 30 September 1888.* Kampen: J. H. Bos, 1888.

———. *Een korte schets van mijn leven* (typoscript), 1906. H. Bavinck Archive, no. 346, folder 444. Amsterdam: Historische Documentatiecentrum.

———. *Feeststoffen* (voor het Kerstfeest en voor het Oud- en Nieuwjaar). Kampen: G. Ph. Zalsman, 1900.

———. *Feeststoffen* (voor het Paaschfeest). Kampen: G. Ph. Zalsman, 1901.

Beets, Nicolaas. *De Gedichten van Nicholaas Beets.* Gent: H. Hoste, 1848.

Bilderdijk, Willem. *De Dieren: Dichtstuk.* Amsterdam: P. den Hengst en Zoon, 1817.

———. *Krekelzangen.* Eerste Deel. Rotterdam: J. Immerzeel Junior, 1822.

Bolt, John. *Bavinck on the Christian Life: Following Jesus in Faithful Service.* Wheaton: Crossway, 2015.

Bowring, John. *Sketch of the Language and Literature of Holland.* Amsterdam: Diederichs Brothers, 1829.

Bremmer, R. *Herman Bavinck en zijn tijdgenoten.* Kampen: Kok, 1966.

Calvin, John. *Lettres françaises.* Edited by J. Bonnet. 2 vols. Paris: Mayrueis, 1854.

de Bruijn, Jan, and George Harinck, eds. *Een Leidse vriendschap.* Baarn: Ten Have, 1999.

Donner, J. H. *Afgewezen, maar niet teleurgesteld: Toespraak naar 1 Koningen 8:17–19a.* Kampen: G. Ph. Zalsman, 1873.

———. *Lichtstralen van den kandelaar des woords.* Leiden: D. Donner, 1883.

Eglinton, James. *Trinity and Organism: Towards a New Reading of Herman Bavinck's Organic Motif.* London: T&T Clark / Bloomsbury, 2012.

Erdmann, Benno. *Die psychol. Grundlagen der Beziehung zw. Sprechen und Denken.* Archiv für systemat. Philos. herausg. Von Natorp. Neue Folge der Philos. Monatshefte II, 1896.

Gangauf, Theodor. *Des h. Augustinus speculative Lehre von Gott dem Dreieinigen.* Augsburg: Schmidt, 1883.

Giesswein, Alexander. *Die Hauptprobleme der Sprachwissenschaft.* Freiburg: Herder, 1892.

Harinck, George. "'Something That Must Remain, If the Truth Is to Be Sweet and Precious to Us': The Reformed Spirituality of Herman Bavinck." *Calvin Theological Journal* 38 (2003): 248–62.

Hartog, Jan. *Geschiedenis der Predikkunde en de evangelieprediking: in de protestantsche kerk van Nederland.* Amsterdam: Frederik Muller, 1861.

Hedge, Frederic Henry. *Prose Writers of Germany.* New York: C. S. Francis and Company, 1855.

Hepp, Valentijn. *Dr. Herman Bavinck.* Amsterdam: W. Ten Have, 1921.

Janet, Paul. *Traité élémentaire de philosophie: à l'usage des classes.* Paris: Delagrave, 1889.

Jodl, Friedrich. *Lehrbuch der Psychologie.* Stuttgart: J. G. Cotta'sche Buchhandlung Nachfolger GmbH., 1903.

Kruger, Paul. *The Memoirs of Paul Kruger: Four Times President of the South African Republic.* Vol. 2. London: T. Fisher Unwin, 1902.

Kuyper, Abraham. "The Blurring of the Boundaries." *Abraham Kuyper: A Centennial Reader*, edited by James Bratt, 363–402. Grand Rapids: Eerdmans, 1998.

———. *Lectures on Calvinism.* Grand Rapids: Eerdmans, 1931.

———. *Scholarship: Two Convocational Addresses on University Life.* Grand Rapids: Christian's Library Press, 2014.

Laman, H. W., ed. *Wandelen door geloof: overdenkingen van de gereformeerde predikanten.* Netherlands: Gereformeerd Tractaatgenootschap "Filippus," 1930.

Lamennais, Hugues-Félicité Robert de. *Paroles d'un croyant*. Paris: Bibliotheque Nationale, 1897.

Landwehr, J. H. *Prof. Dr. H. Bavinck*. Kampen: J. H. Kok, 1921.

Lindberg, Carter. "The Blood of the Martyrs: The Reformation in the Netherlands." *The European Reformations*. Oxford: Wiley Blackwell, 2010, 282–92.

Luther, Martin. *Martin Luther's Tabletalk*. Edited by William Hazlitt. Fearn, Scotland, UK: Christian Focus Publications, 2003.

Matthews, W. K. "The Japhetic Theory." *The Slavonic and East European Review* 27, no. 68 (December 1948): 172–92.

Müller, Max. *Das Denken im Lichte der Sprache*. Leipzig: Engelmann, 1888.

————. *Vorlesungen über die Wissenschaft der Sprache*. I Serie. 3rd ed. Leipzig: J. Klinkhardt, 1875.

Multatuli. *Ideeën I*. Amsterdam: Funke, 1879.

————. *Max Havelaar, of de koffie-veilingen der Nederlandsche Handel-Maatschappy*. Amsterdam: De Ruyter, 1860.

Nancy, Jean-Luc. *Les Muses*. Paris: Editions Galilée, 1994.

Potgieter, E. J. *De werken*, Deel I. Edited by J. C. Zimmerman. Haarlem: H. D. Tjeenk Willink, 1908.

Rousseau, Jean-Jacques. *Oeuvres complètes de J. J. Rousseau: Emile, Tome II*. Paris: Dupont, 1823.

Rückert, Friedrich. *Die Weisheit des Brahmannen: ein Lehrgedicht in Bruchstücken*. Vol. 4. Leipzig: Weidmann, 1841.

Schillebeeckx, Edward. *The Collected Works of Edward Schillebeeckx Volume 4: World and Church*. London: T&T Clark, 2014.

————. *For the Sake of the Gospel*. New York: Crossroad, 1990.

Schleyer, Johann Martin, Alfred Kirchhoff, and Klas August Linderfelt. *Volapük: Easy Method of Acquiring the Universal Language*. C. N. Caspar, 1888.

Sincerus. *De Kanselontluistering in de Ned. Herv. Kerk tijdens 17de en 18de eeuw aangewezen en gestaafd*. Amsterdam, 1852.

Stöckl, Albert. *Lehrbuch der Philosophie*. 6th ed. I. Mainz: F. Kirchheim, 1887.

Theremin, Franz. *Demosthenes en Massillon: Eene bijdrage tot de geschiedenis der welsprekendheid.* Translated by J. Schade. 's-Gravenhage: J. M. van 't Haaff, 1847.

Van Oosterzee, Johannes Jacobus. *Practische theologie: een handboek voor jeugdige godgeleerden,* Deel 1. Utrecht: Kemink, 1877.

Van Prinsterer, Guillaume Groen. *Groen van Prinsterer's Lectures on Unbelief and Revolution.* Translated by Harry van Dyke. Jordan Station, Canada: Wedge Publishing Foundation, 1989.

———. *Ongeloof en revolutie. Eene reeks van historische voorlezingen.* Leiden: S. and J. Luchtmans, 1847.

Van Vloten, J. *Nederlandsch dicht en ondicht der negentiende eeuw.* Deventer: A. ter Gunne, 1861.

Wit, Willem J. de, "'Will I remain standing?': A Cathartic Reading of Herman Bavinck." *The Bavinck Review* 2 (2011): 25.

INDEX OF NAMES

INDEX OF SUBJECTS